UN-BOSSED
DREAMS, HUSTLE TO 'FREEDOM OF CHOICE'

BEGINNERS ROADMAP TO FINANCIAL FREEDOM, WEALTH BUILDING & MINDSET SHIFT

HITESH K. PAHUJA

Clever Fox®
PUBLISHING
Chennai • Bangalore

CLEVER FOX PUBLISHING
Chennai, India

Published by CLEVER FOX PUBLISHING 2026

ISBN: 978-93-7500-097-6

The book is dedicated to:

My Mother, who taught me contentment, gratitude, and humility

My life partner, Neha, who stood by my side in every situation

My children, Nehit & Aarshia whose unconditional love & innocence continues to inspire me

CHAPTERS

Context & Preface

FINANCIAL FREEDOM DOES NOT EQUAL RETIREMENT

Before we begin, let us very briefly dwell into the concepts of Financial Freedom (FF) and Retirement for the avoidance of any confusion as we go.

Financial Freedom is having enough income and/or assets that cover your living expenses without relying on a job or anyone else, *regardless of age or work status (This is the key difference, so you could be Financially independent at 30 but might still retire at 60)*. In FF, the goal is to free yourself from the need to work for money, allowing you to choose whether to work, retire early, pursue passion projects, or do anything else with your time or search for your 'Ikigai' / life's purpose.

On the other hand, **Retirement** is a phase of life when you stop working full-time (usually at a traditional retirement age around 60, reducing with time though) and rely on your pension, investments, or social security for your expenses. Retirement planning is generally done through savings plans, pension schemes, mutual funds, insurance products, etc.

In typical Indian households, Financial Freedom (FF) is seldom part of any dinner table conversation of families. While most working professionals discuss the importance of higher education, career moves, savings, retirement plans, etc. with their kids, but not really a faster way to reach financial freedom. Even for the better planned ones, goals would have something around retirement, but not necessarily around Financial Freedom.

Unfortunately, this is true even for many financial planners/investment advisors who focus on retirement as a goal but rarely include Financial Freedom as an interim goal before full-time retirement. The mindset needs to change, considering the world we are living in and the rate of change around us. Financial Freedom is far more important goal than retirement, and it's important for all of us start prioritising it.

While the majority of us confuse Financial Freedom with early retirement, these are different life stages, and ideally, Financial Freedom should precede retirement. It is quite common to see people equate Retirement and Financial Freedom; however, both are fundamentally different and hence deserve a different space in your goal-based planning. For some people chasing early retirement, FF & retirement planning might be common goals, but if you don't want to retire early, FF will have a whole different meaning for you. In fact, I have seen people who have not achieved financial freedom even at retirement and remain dependent on children/family, etc. Therefore, financial freedom as a concept needs a lot of emphasis for most working professionals with or without early retirement goals.

Having said the above, FF makes your retirement plan much easier and you would be far better prepared. In fact, you might not need a significant effort for retirement as a goal and may need minor tweaking to your financial plans if you wish to completely stop working after achieving FF. High saving rate and building a passive income stream (through investments, rental income, businesses, royalties, professional pursuits, etc.) are some of the ways to become financially independent. Financial Freedom can be achieved before the traditional retirement age and requires disciplined saving, investing, reducing expenses, and often diversifying income sources.

Here is a quick table to make this crystal clear for all of us:

Retirement	Financial Freedom
Usually linked to a specific retirement age	Can be at any age
Typically means stopping full-time work	Freedom to choose – work on passion projects, start-up idea, teaching, Travel etc.
Security in old age	Freedom and choice at any life stage

Retirement	Financial Freedom
Long-term accumulation with an end-goal	Sustainable income-generating assets & cash flow

Key Takeaways

- *Financial Freedom should be a must-have goal in one's financial journey and is not necessarily retirement*
- *Financial freedom can be achieved at any stage of life and helps you work on your passion or just take a break from your work routine to explore*
- *It can be achieved with disciplined investing &/or diversifying income sources*

Context & Preface

ORIGIN OF THIS BOOK & SOME CAVEATS

Life teaches you many lessons, some as part of your professional journey, while others come from experiences in personal life, some easy to adapt, while some are not so easy to implement, some with consequences (financial or non-financial), and some that will just make you wiser without any consequential damage.

If I were to look back and list some of these learnings of my life, the idea behind writing this book would emerge as one of the top few key learnings of my life. First and foremost, would be due to the following questions that I have often asked myself and have seen most people struggle with. Let me try to prompt some thinking in your mind with these not so easy to answer questions before we move forward:

- How many of us actually wanted to do what we are doing for a living and might have chosen a different path if making money wasn't the only criterion?
- If you were to apply Ikigai - Japanese philosophy that combines "life" ('Iki') and "worth" ('gai') to mean your "reason for being", would you still be doing what you are doing? Do you know your Ikigai?

Here are the 4 questions that Ikigai as a concept wants us to answer:

- ***What you love:*** *Your passion and what brings you joy. ('Passion')*
- ***What you are good at:*** *Your skills and talents. ('Vocation')*
- ***What the world needs:*** *Your potential contribution to others and society. ('Mission')*
- ***What you can be paid for:*** *How you can sustain yourself financially. ('Profession')*

While most of us will struggle to answer these questions about our 'Ikigai' with conviction and clarity at the beginning of our careers (in fact, even a lot later in life as well), but many would at least conclude that they would have loved doing or trying something else given a choice. While some of us are lucky to find our purpose at some stage, most would need to try a few things before we could reach a reasonable conclusion around it. To attempt this soul-searching mission, you need freedom to spend time as per your wish, rather than a fixed schedule or well-paying engagement. This freedom of 'choice' is the first factor that has always emerged as the number one reason for me to think of financial freedom as a concept – now, while there are multiple other reasons that emerged over time (explained later in this book), this one reason remains at the top of my mind.

The other related reason this book came into being is the path to financial freedom, i.e., dealing with money or making decisions related to personal finance. During my numerous interactions with people of my age group and the generations younger to me (especially the ones with comparatively lower financial exposure), one thing that always stood out for me was the extremely low level of awareness about personal finance in general, which led to their inability to rationally make decisions around spending, saving, and most significantly around investing. While things are improving and some curious youngsters understand this subject more than I did at that age, I find there is still a very large gap in this area that needs a significant amount of knowledge sharing.

Even when I look at my own journey with money, I have made significant mistakes by way of irrational financial decisions (or rather blunders) over time, despite being a finance professional. Having made so many mistakes, which almost derailed my financial plans, I realised the importance of appropriate guidance or a correct perspective in one's life, specifically when it comes to personal finance decisions. This is the other important reason the book was conceptualised, as it allows me to share some perspective on financial freedom as well as basic financial literacy, which is directly linked to saving as well as investing – two key personal finance decisions that one takes at various stages of life.

While I have personally experienced the need for some guidance or handholding around both of these issues (having a goal of freedom of choice and personal finance principles for a more meaningful/fulfilling life) and have learnt through experience and failures, the need for these themes has remained almost static in all my interactions with people of different backgrounds. Over the last 25 years of my working career, I have seen and met many with a feeling that they probably are stuck on the wrong path and would have loved to do something different or more meaningful. However, they lack the resources as well as the courage to step aside from a career that pays the bills. More importantly, they lack the conviction to take some decisive steps to make this a reality at some stage.

While it may not be possible for everyone to identify their 'Ikigai' at the beginning of one's career, nor should the need to earn 'livelihood' be ignored, however there is no reason that one should not aim for this freedom of choice at some stage of the career if life gives one a chance.

One of the other factors, which is more behavioural than anything else, is our constant desire to live someone else's life and the urge to accumulate more wealth. While there may not be anything wrong with constant upgrade and accumulation, provided you are enjoying this process, and if you are not, you better figure out what makes you happier. We keep enhancing our wants and continue to spend based on social norms rather than stopping and reflecting if we actually enjoy what we do.

We all give a lot of importance to career, growth, saving, retirement, etc., but generally don't prioritise Freedom of choice as a goal which could give you an opportunity to live life on your own terms or explore and experience some paths in search of your 'Ikigai'.

As I started to reflect on all the above, it became increasingly clear that this one idea could help the younger generation (specifically people in their 20s to 30s) do a few things better than I did, i.e.

- Appreciate the importance of this life goal early on
- Avoid mistakes or behavioural issues while dealing with money

- Own their time at some stage of life &
- Build courage to live a life of their choice

This reflection leads me to believe that a practical reference guide (not a prescription definitely) would help the younger generation handle these life situations or goals better. Hence, one of the first things I thought of completing the moment I took a short break from full time job (after 25 years of working career) was this book.

What does this offer

Core idea behind this book is to ignite the need for financial freedom in people younger than me and make sure they develop a plan to achieve it much earlier than I did. Eventually, helping them have freedom of choice at some stage.

We live in a world that often dictates our choices and this book attempts to provide a path to take back that control. Financial freedom is the power to choose your own path, free from the anxiety of making ends meet. You will discover that financial freedom is not only about a specific net worth, but about having enough resources to live your life according to your values and goals, whether that means pursuing a passion, taking a risk, travelling, or simply enjoying more time with loved ones.

So, the book attempts to lay down the rational for including financial freedom as one of the long-term goals for saving & investing (i.e. Business Case

for Financial Freedom), provides some high-level guidance or direction to make a beginning as well as staying consistent with a plan (i.e. Journey of Financial Freedom) and eventually helping one use wealth to enable choices & opportunities rather than just for accumulation (i.e. The End Game).

The book should help you develop a practical step-by-step roadmap rather than give you a get-rich-quick scheme. It should help you develop a clear, actionable plan to build wealth by investing wisely. By the end of this journey, you will have a clear understanding of your own financial mindset and a concrete strategy for building a life that isn't limited by your bank account. Get ready to unlock the freedom to live life on your own terms.

I have tried to use my own learnings along the way, which might help you do more of what has helped me and less of what was a mistake in hindsight. If this helps some people become slightly wiser, the book would have achieved its intended purpose.

Some Caveats & Caution

This book is for information & education purposes and should not be considered as a prescription for your financial planning process. The book does not guarantee financial success, and financial markets involve inherent risks; outcomes can be unpredictable.

The importance of professional help in developing your own personal financial plan cannot be overruled by any such guiding document, and it is extremely critical to rely on professional advice for financial decisions.

The book is a result of many personal mistakes and therefore might carry some biases (though I have tried to be as objective as possible) of my own decision principles, and therefore I would strongly recommend that this be used as a guideline document and not as a prescription. Given our diverse situations, it is next to impossible for any such book to prescribe a specific plan for individual situations.

The best way to use this work is to understand the need (for Financial Freedom) as well as the approach, and then work on creating a specific plan that matches your personal situation. Further, while I have focused on FF as a goal in this book but the same approach and investing principles can be applied to any goal based investing e.g. Child Education, Retirement planning etc. Hence, this knowledge should help you understand the basics of long term wealth creation irrespective of the goal.

Lastly, it isn't a "get rich quick" scheme, and building financial security is a gradual, long-term process.

I have used Financial Freedom (FF) and Financial Independence (FI) interchangeably at various places in the book – Both in my view are two different terms for the same stage of life.

Key Takeaways

- *Everyone deserves freedom of choice for a soul-searching mission and should focus on this goal from early on*
- *This book is an attempt to help the reader develop a path for financial freedom and should not be considered as a prescription*
- *The book does not guarantee financial success in any form, and financial markets involve inherent risks*
- *If you truly aspire for Financial Freedom, you should stop constantly enhancing your wants based on social norms and rather reflect at some stage if you actually enjoy what you do*

Context & Preface

a. *Financial Freedom isn't Retirement*

b. *Origin of this Book and Some Caveats*

c. *Indian Psychology & Historical Beliefs About Money & Investing*

INDIAN PSYCHOLOGY & HISTORICAL BELIEFS ABOUT MONEY & INVESTING

The Indian psychology about money is more about Security than Freedom. In typical Indian households, money is rarely discussed as a tool for freedom, and rather related to Security, Social respect (which also means display of wealth sometimes takes precedence over saving), and risk mitigation against any mishaps.

Some of these beliefs about money also stem from a lack of social security frameworks, financial instability, and uncertainty about earning/income.

There are quite a few good things as well, which emanate from this psychology, but it also leads to some basic flaws which impact the financial freedom journey of any individual. Hence, it's important to discuss both the good and the ugly before we can figure out the sweet spots.

Here are some of the good things about this psychology, which in some ways help the financial freedom journey:

- **Saving over spending**: Given this psychology, Indians are generally better savers than many in the west which originates from a lack of social security mechanism. This helps as you start your financial freedom journey. As they say, Money saved is money earned.
- **Obsession with Gold**: Most Indian households (more specifically, the females) are obsessed with possessing gold as a form of family wealth or security. Traditionally, this has been largely in the form of ornaments, which lose a lot of value given the making charges and come with the risks of safekeeping, etc. Having said that, this habit has still led to significant wealth creation for Indians, with the gold prices rising sharply over time, and specifically in the last few years. This, in my view, is again something that, if modified with changing context (e.g., buy pure gold in addition to ornaments), could help any Indian to fast-track their financial freedom journey.

Here are some of the not-so-good things which in some ways derail the financial freedom journey:

- **Wealth Accumulation**: The Indian mindset has traditionally valued saving and accumulation as a core element of financial behaviour. This habit originates from centuries of cultural, economic, and social influences. Indians have long associated wealth with security, stability, and social standing rather than conspicuous consumption. This ingrained habit of accumulation has shaped the country's personal finance patterns and continues to evolve in the modern economy.

Historically, limited access to formal financial systems and volatile economic conditions made precautionary saving a necessity. Gold, land, and real estate emerged as preferred stores of value — tangible, trusted, and often inherited across generations. Even today, India remains one of the largest global consumers of gold, reflecting this deep cultural affinity toward asset accumulation.

However, a gradual shift from saving to investing is emerging. Rising incomes, improved financial literacy, and digital access have enabled more Indians to explore market-linked instruments such as mutual funds, equities, and retirement products. Systematic Investment Plans (SIPs) have become emblematic of this change — blending the old habit of disciplined saving with the new mindset of wealth creation. As of late 2025, SIP inflows exceed ₹28,000 crore monthly, showcasing how traditional thrift is finding modern expression through financialization.

Despite this progress, the Indian saver still tends to prioritize safety and liquidity over risk and return. Bank deposits, insurance, and small savings schemes continue to dominate household portfolios. The transition from accumulation to productive investing remains uneven across income levels, regions, and generations.

In essence, the Indian accumulation habit represents both a strength and a challenge. It anchors financial resilience and long-term security but can also limit potential wealth growth if not channelized effectively. The next phase of India's financial journey lies in transforming this cultural instinct to save into a more strategic approach to invest, compound, and create wealth — ensuring that the habit of accumulation evolves with the nation's economic aspirations.

- **Fixed income over Growth Assets**: While Indians have been traditionally reasonable savers, most of us have been risk-averse and have preferred fixed income instruments, which barely cover inflation, or rather most of the time don't cover inflation over a longer period of time. As a result, savings of Indian households haven't kept pace with the rising cost of living, and the money has been losing value. As per RBI data of 2023, Mutual funds hold about 6% of household savings vs. about 45% parked in Bank Deposits, which isn't ideal for the long-term growth of money. This is improving, though, with every passing year.
- **Obsession with Real Estate**: Indians have a very high liking for real estate as an asset class, which, with all its benefits over a longer time period, has multiple limitation including extreme illiquidity. For decades, real estate has been the ultimate status symbol and safest investment. Owning a home has been the first

financial goal for most Indians. Due to rising prices, lower rentals, and illiquidity, the younger generation is rethinking real estate, but it remains an emotional need for most. In my own view, owning real estate isn't bad, but over investing into this asset class can have varied results and is not ideal for most due to issues like illiquidity.

- **Treating Insurance Policies and ULIPs as Investment instruments**: Most of us would have faced the issue of our parents' reliance on an insurance policy advisor who ended up selling multiple policies to our parents, with real returns in the longer run much lower than fixed rate instruments with some negligible insurance coverage built into it.

  While this has been a huge issue, the awareness levels to avoid this are still very low. Most people end up parking funds in multiple policies without even looking at the returns in the longer term. The best way to evaluate any insurance policy that has an element of saving/investment built into it is to look at the returns over the life of the policy. More on this when we look at various investment options in subsequent sections of this book.
- **DIY (Do it yourself) Investing**: Most Indians believe they don't need any help in planning and executing their financial goals. This psyche is less driven by overconfidence and more by the fact that most are not comfortable sharing their financial status or the details

of their savings with others. This has led to higher reliance on safer assets like bank deposits, which has, over time, impacted real returns.

While things are changing and more participation in the growth assets is visible, and Mutual funds are becoming a preferred mode of investment for many these days, but here is what one needs to keep in mind to avoid the pitfalls of historical wisdom in Indian households:

- **Avoid Fixed Income Instruments for long-term goals:** Goals like child education, financial freedom, Retirement, etc., need investment in growth/risk assets given the time horizon. Typically, these goals are 15-20 years away as you start, so there is enough runway to allow your money to grow and bear the downturn cycles, if any. Here is some data showing the long term returns of various asset classes, including Equities.

Indian Equities **have** outperformed **all** other asset classes over the long run; ~15% returns **over** 20 years — FundsIndia

Index	Compound Annualized Returns (%) – as on 29-Feb-2024					
	1Y	3Y	5Y	10Y	15Y	20Y
India – Equity (Nifty 50 TRI)	28.5	16.2	16.7	14.7	16.2	14.8
US – Equity (S&P 500 TRI in INR)	30.4	16.2	18.4	16.0	19.8	13.3
Gold (in INR)	12.6	9.9	12.6	7.5	8.7	11.9
Real Estate*	3.9	5.0	4.8	4.4	6.6	8.2
Debt*	7.4	5.5	6.6	7.3	7.3	7.3

Returns as on 29-Feb-2024

Source: Funds India – Wealth Conversations August 2024

If you compare the returns of Debt and Equity, you will realise that Debt (generally fixed income) barely beats inflation, whereas equity gave almost double the returns in the longer term. Having said that, historical returns are no guarantee of similar performance in the future. However, given the GDP growth rates in India and the developing nature of our economy, one can assume to get inflation-beating returns over the next few decades.

Hence, investing aggressively in equities for all long-term goals is almost essential for any young professional.

- **Never mix Insurance Coverage and Investment**: Both of these objectives need very different strategy and mixing these two as part of a single policy generally isn't recommended. This has been another myth that Indian psychology has carried for ages – There has been a strong belief that Insurance policies are vehicles of Investment while in the longer term, their returns rarely beat inflation. Most of the insurance policies that are sold as an investing vehicle end up giving mid-single digit returns over a longer time horizon and making you poorer in terms of cost-of-living over time. As a thumb rule, avoid buying insurance policies with money-back plans, or if you were to, talk to an expert (not the agent who has a conflict of interest) and try getting the returns over the life of the policy. In most cases, the answer would be a single-digit return, not even beating the existing inflation. Further, the risk coverage (or life cover) in most of these money-back policies would be extremely low and may not cover the family in case of any eventuality.

- **Treat Gold as an asset class beyond just jewellery**: Buy jewellery to the extent you need, but don't buy this for dumping in your bank locker. Gold should be part of the investment strategy, but use better instruments like Exchange Traded Funds (ETF), Gold bonds, Gold Mutual Funds as an investment rather than jewellery. We will discuss how much gold makes sense in subsequent sections.
- **Weddings:** Indians love to spend money on 2 important life milestones, i.e. Marriage and building a home (sometimes out of family pressures). While there is no harm in celebrating your wedding or other important life milestones with your friends & family, don't go overboard with the display of wealth. I have seen people taking personal loans to have a lavish wedding, which has never made sense to me.

  Morgan Housel's quote below explains the idea better than any further explanation:

“

“Spending money to show people how much money you have is the fastest way to have less money.”

– Morgan Housel,

The Psychology of Money (2020).

Key Takeaways

- *Learn about growth investing and avoid fixed income security for longer term wealth creation*
- *Gold & Real Estate need to be evaluated based on returns as well as liquidity and should generally not be significant part of your investment strategy*
- *Display of wealth is the fastest way to lose money in the long term*
- *Insurance and Investment are very different needs– don't mix the two*
- *A good wealth advisor can add a lot of value to the process of saving & investing – Invest in one with 'no-conflict'.*

More on these principles in subsequent sections.

Retirement is a choice but Financial Freedom should not be – Delaying this life goal is delaying Life of your Choice

The 'Business Case' for Financial Freedom

a. Chasing 'moving goal posts' to 'jumping the treadmill' – A real story

b. Gaining control of your time

c. Changing employment scenario

d. Prepare for the 'Pandemic'

Why Financial Freedom needs to be a key goal in your Life journey.

Financial freedom actually goes beyond having wealth — it's about having control, choice, and peace of mind in how you live. When money ceases to be a constant source of worry, emotional well-being naturally improves. In a world where financial stress is one of the most common causes of anxiety and relationship strain, achieving financial independence can be deeply liberating.

The first and most direct impact of financial freedom is the reduction of financial stress. When individuals have an emergency fund, manageable or no debt, and a steady stream of passive or investment income, they no longer operate in a state of fear about bills, job loss, or unexpected expenses. This sense of stability reduces chronic stress hormones like cortisol and promotes a calmer, more confident state of mind.

Secondly, financial freedom fosters autonomy and life satisfaction. When people are not bound by paycheck-to-paycheck living, they can make choices aligned with their values — whether that means pursuing a passion project, spending more time with family, or even taking a sabbatical. **The ability to say no to what doesn't align with one's goals is one of the purest forms of emotional freedom.**

Many of us might feel that we would want to continue working till late in life and may not really feel the need to plan for an interim goal of financial freedom, but here is a different perspective. Even if you aspire to continue working in your job or whatever profession you have, financial freedom gives you a very different confidence mentally and emotionally, which is, at times, priceless.

Financial freedom allows you to take risks. Once you are financially free (whether fully or partially), you would be able to take career risks more easily. Money allows you to take such a plunge without fear of failure, given the safety net you have created. This is true both before and after hitting the freedom number – I have personally taken a lot of career risks with different roles, given my spending patterns were always controlled, and I never had unmanageable debt (except at the beginning of my career for a brief time when I went overboard on real estate)– fear of failure in anything new is absolutely normal, but you should not fear the repercussions if something did not work out.

You start to experience much lesser stress in your job once you realise you have covered your needs and don't have to fully depend on the active earnings. Having said that, someone might argue that it has the potential of making you complacent in your work routine, but that is more a personal trait than an outcome of achieving financial freedom. In my view, your view of the world and your way of experiencing things would change significantly once you know that you, as well as your family's needs, are already addressed.

It also enhances self-esteem and confidence. The discipline required to build wealth — budgeting, investing, and planning — reinforces a sense of control and accomplishment. This, in turn, nurtures emotional resilience and a growth mindset, making individuals less reactive to external pressures.

Financial independence can further improve relationships and social connections. Money-related conflicts are among the top reasons for tension within families and couples. With a secure financial foundation, these conflicts often diminish, allowing more honest communication, shared goals, and emotional closeness.

Ultimately, financial freedom creates the space to live deliberately — to focus on purpose, creativity, and relationships rather than survival. It doesn't guarantee happiness, but it removes one of the largest barriers to it. Emotional well-being thrives when people feel secure, in control, and free to live life on their own terms — and that's exactly what financial freedom offers.

CHASING 'MOVING GOAL POSTS' TO 'JUMPING THE TREADMILL'

– A Real Story

The story starts in the early 90s.

It's a story of a typical middle-class boy who grew up in multiple small cities in North India owing to a transferable job of his parents. While he was growing, the Family moved cities almost every alternate year, given the nature of the job. That meant multiple schools with exposure to varying lifestyles of people around in each city, some lavish and some not so lavish. This journey continued, leaving some impressions on him before the family finally settled in Patiala, where he studied till graduation. His family was a service class family with a middle-class lifestyle, which meant no luxuries and the only thing that was guaranteed at any cost was the education of kids, good food & lots of love – everything else needed years of planning, so he kept getting inspired by even a small amount of luxury around him.

During one of the days while his Dad was posted in Amritsar (a comparatively richer city in Punjab), he was driven around by an acquaintance of his father who was a well-off business man and owned a Hindustan Contessa (the classic rich man's car in olden days) – This was the first time, he experienced luxury and started visualising if he could someday own it!

The family also had some relatives in Delhi, due to which they made occasional trips to the city, which would mostly be during summer holidays. As a child who studied in multiple 'B' towns and was occasionally exposed to the lifestyle of Delhi, the biggest ambition he carried was to somehow move to a metro city, get a good job, earn some money, and be able to afford a house/ apartment in a Metro. A car of his own was also a distant, hidden dream, though it was too big to acknowledge at this stage.

The comparatively flamboyant lifestyle of Delhi as a city attracted him in many ways, and it became an ambition over time. Given the ambitions and attraction towards metro living, he would look for opportunities to get exposed to the settings. One of these opportunities came in the form of coaching for a professional course, which he had started pursuing along with his graduation. During 1997-98, he came to Delhi to attend coaching classes for this professional course. These were morning classes organised by the Institute, and most of the teachers were professionals working in corporates at junior or middle management roles who would do part-time teaching out of passion or to make some extra money (maybe for fast tracking their financial freedom journey as well – though he did not have an inclination towards this term by then).

One of the tutors in these classes (let's name him Mr Singh, who was in his late 40s / early 50s) was working with a reasonably well-known brand, would come driving a car to the Institute, and was always very well dressed & would often wear a tie. His personality, as well as his visual appearance, inspired this young guy from a small town. One of these days, Mr Singh started sharing his journey to say that he came from a small-town couple of decades ago and was now staying in Delhi in an upper-middle-class neighbourhood in his own house. That's the first time, he thought to himself, that if he could somehow copy his tutor's lifestyle, he would be sorted forever. So that's the level of financial ambition he started with, but then life happened, comparisons started, and goal posts kept changing, and dreams became bigger before something changed!

Having visualised what success could be and also thinking of this as a stretch goal, he started working towards this. Now, this was just a beginning and would have meant a decent job and a satisfied life in a middle-class neighbourhood with a car. But then, as I said, life happened, and as he moved to Delhi to pursue further studies, he started getting exposed to the life of Delhi. Over time, He started to think, maybe there is more to catch up than just to imitate Mr. Singh. This was the first-time comparisons influenced his thinking of what he wanted in life to be successful but for now, he did not change his goal post (not due to modesty but because for him, his tutor's lifestyle was still a stretch goal given his starting point of a small town). He had to become a permanent resident of Metro City first before he could stretch his goals. So, he still felt, wearing a tie on his neck, having the badge of a good job and a self-driven car driven into his own home parking in the city would be good enough to prove his worth in society!

As he started chasing his dreams after moving to Delhi, Serendipity helped him at every stage. Soon after finishing his higher studies, he started with his first job in his early 20s and bought his own Car (at age 24 in 2003) with a low-cost loan provided by his employer. The car turned out to be slightly bigger than his tutor. His employers provided him with a nice apartment in an upmarket area of the National Capital Region (NCR), i.e., used to describe areas in and around Delhi, which was beyond his imagination. This is the time he started feeling he had arrived. This feeling stayed for some time till Comparisons started again, and the guy wanted to run even faster.

This was a job with a public sector undertaking with a lot of job security but lower money or growth potential in the short run (again comparatively), so he started to think that he should look at moving to the private sector, which offered better rewards financially and faster growth. He wasn't alone with that thinking – In fact, he was 10th to leave this sought-after public-sector role in a batch of 13 individuals who were picked up by the firm through a rigorous campus recruitment process across India.

The decision was again driven largely by peer comparisons, as his friends/batch mates who had joined the private sector were financially growing faster, so he succumbed to the peer pressure. He joined a private sector consulting firm with a higher cash salary (much lower perks, though), which meant travelling about 3 hours every day to chase bigger dreams, but he kept going.

This chase kept getting aggressive, and that meant growing roles/responsibilities and higher salaries, which came with higher expectations and work pressures. One job after the other, his career moved way beyond his own expectations. Fast forward to the 2020s, he became a CXO and eventually occupied the corner office as the CEO of the India Business of a large MNC.

While this kept going for about 25 odd years, from early 2000 till 2025, something started changing in the background simultaneously. Despite all the comforts and a sought-after well-paying job, he started experiencing a change in his thinking and questioned the chase for more sometime in his late 30s or early 40s. He started to visualise a life at his own pace, not driven by deadlines, doing something he would love doing, etc., and asked himself if jumping this high-speed treadmill was ever an option. He had to answer 3 key questions before he could even think of something that radical, not working in a 9-5 role and the most critical of the 3 was number 1 below:

1. Enough Financial Resources to take that risk of leaving the job
2. Manage peer pressure and social comparisons
3. Find something meaningful & satisfying without money being the only criterion – maybe his 'Ikigai'

He quickly realised that not only was he not ready yet, but he never even imagined the possibility of this change of heart while in his 20s and hence never specifically planned for it. Having said that, given that he came from a middle-class upbringing, he was a reasonable saver all along, so he had some corpus to fall back on, which wasn't sufficient for 'freedom', so he had to do something different. He started saving aggressively and made some choices in life, which meant prioritising the freedom goal more than anything else.

He jumped the treadmill in late 2025 with courage & conviction that he needed a break to reflect on last 25 years of working career and finish a few dream projects i.e. write a book and finish his mountain home that he started building couple of years ago – it's been a mini break for him to experience life at his own pace for some time and see if this is what is more satisfying than the regular 9-5 role - There are no guarantees that this is what would be most rewarding and he would not pick up another regular engagement but one thing is clear that this break has been liberating and has been instrumental in changing his perspective towards work and life!

The story is a real story of the author and is based on true events, and this could be you in your 40s ! if you notice in the story, the change of heart was extremely contrasting - it started with ever-increasing ambitions with 'chasing more' and ended with 'Freedom of choice with less'.

The idea of narrating this story to you as the reader is to emphasise the point that it would be foolish for anyone to assume that what excites you in your 20s and your 30s would keep you equally engaged in your 40s. The need to achieve financial freedom is real to make sure you are not stuck with a career path or work routine that you no longer desire (and human desires change every few months if not every few days 😊)!

During this 25-years of my working career, I have met multiple people and am yet to find anyone who is happy working in a 9-5 setting forever. If you look around, this change of heart is actually not very unusual with many people in their late 30s or 40s.

Some of the most common reasons could be to do something of their own, a start-up idea, or spend more time with family, or could just be to travel more frequently! The challenge is that no one can visualise this in their 20s as life starts with chasing dreams for most, which is absolutely fine, but then if you don't plan for financial freedom sometime in your 20s, you may miss out on your start-up idea or miss the opportunity to take a mini break to write a book or to travel!

My own reasons for considering a break post FF were more to experience life at a slow pace and focus on some of my personal priorities, including attempting this book. One of the biggest driving forces behind this decision is also my belief that one should not regret later that you did not attempt searching for your Ikigai.

Last but not the least, once you realise that the time on earth for each of us is limited, you start to prioritise your own desires vs. societal needs like better titles, more money, etc. So, this is another reason which lot of times lets people choose freedom over more paying careers available out there. The reasons could be multiple, with some wanting to do a start-up, while others wanting to travel, and a few others wanting to just discover their purpose in life. Irrespective of the reason, to let go of a life dependent on a paycheck, you must first decide and then plan for an independent one.

As Marcus Aurelius (Stoic philosopher) put it very aptly:

> *"You could leave life right now. Let that determine what you do and say and think."*

In most cases, this realisation comes later in life, and if you haven't planned for financial freedom, it becomes almost impossible to take this call.

Key Takeaways

- *Human preferences evolve, and financial freedom can prepare you for your changing preferences*
- *Time on earth for each of us is limited; prioritise your own desires without worrying about societal pressures*
- *Financial Freedom enhances one's risk taking ability and might even act as a catalyst to your performance – whether in your regular job or something unique you are attempting*

The 'Business Case' for Financial Freedom

a. Chasing 'moving goal posts' to 'jumping the treadmill' – A real story

b. Gaining control of your time

c. Changing employment scenario

d. Prepare for the 'Pandemic'

GAINING CONTROL OF YOUR TIME

There is a quote from the famous book, Psychology of Money (by Morgan Housel), which has stuck with me for some time - here is an extract:

> *"Use money to gain control over your time - the ability to do what you want, when you want and with whom you want, for as long as you want to, pays the highest dividend that exists in finance."*

If there is one concept / soft skill that is rarely discussed amongst working professionals and their families/ children, it's the importance of Financial Freedom in one's career/life. Now, this isn't new but has a whole new meaning in the current era with changing lifestyles, stressful / shortened careers, and personal aspirations. While I realised this much later in life but am glad I did and started making attempts towards this goal.

There could be multiple reasons why one would want to achieve financial freedom by a certain age, and many of these reasons are more voluntary, but there are some external factors as well, which are making this goal increasingly critical for every working professional.

Voluntary reasons could be your desire to own your time, i.e., flexibility to do whatever you like without worrying about financial rewards attached to the same. In most cases, careers are made based on what makes more money and is in demand as a skill than what you really would enjoy doing during your lifetime.

Having said that, it's important to earn a livelihood and hence prioritising the paying skills is great to begin with. However, as time passes and we fulfil our baseline desires, our desire to do what we wanted to do might start to overpower our thinking, and we may want to leave working for money, which is what leads to a change of heart for many. Now, in such situations, without proper planning, it might be impossible to follow your passion.

In my own case, Financial Freedom was never part of my core agenda till my late 30s, and then suddenly I started to question my own choices. Not that I had clarity on what I wanted to do, or I wasn't doing well in my career, but just that I wasn't too keen to continue working in a 9-5 environment till 60. This is when I seriously started thinking about investing for this goal. Fortunately, I was always a reasonable saver, and hence I repositioned some of my corpus towards this goal and consciously started working towards enhancing the same to achieve FF.

Though, in hindsight, with proper planning, this could have been much smoother.

HSBC's recent survey during 2025 found that Mini Retirements are Gaining Popularity

- The survey found that **85% of Indian respondents** believe taking a mini retirement enhances their quality of life. Nearly **half of the respondents** plan to take two to three mini retirements, each lasting up to a year.
- These breaks are often used to pursue personal passions, spend time with family, or travel.
- Younger generations are leading this trend: **64% of Gen Z** and **58% of millennials** in India are in favour of mini retirements.
- These groups are more inclined to take intentional career breaks every six years to realign their personal and professional goals.

This shift suggests that Financial Freedom is increasingly viewed as a tool for achieving personal fulfilment rather than solely as a means to retire from work. The trend towards mini retirements reflects a broader desire for work-life balance and the pursuit of personal passions.

Key Takeaways

- *Using money to gain control over your time may be the best use of money in your lifetime*
- *There is no harm in normalising mini-breaks for a more fulfilled and meaningful life*

The 'Business Case' for Financial Freedom

a. Chasing 'moving goal posts' to 'jumping the treadmill' – A real story

b. Gaining control of your time

c. Changing employment scenario

d. Prepare for the 'Pandemic'

CHANGING EMPLOYMENT SCENARIO

The other equally pressing reason (if not more) is the rapid change in the employment scenario across the world. The World is changing faster than we ever imagined, and careers are becoming more fragile with every passing year. Reducing dependency on a sole source of income and having a nest egg could not be more essential than in current times.

Given the pace of change and the advent of Artificial Intelligence, the job market would continue to evolve, and more people would eventually have to upskill or live with the risk of being taken out of the working population. Re-learning would be an option, but not everyone might be able to adapt to the rate of change.

A lot of routine, repetitive tasks are being automated. Jobs once thought to be "stable" are being redefined or eliminated. More companies are relying on contract workers, freelance, gig workers, or temporary staffing instead of a large full-time permanent workforce. This gives employers more flexibility but means workers have less predictability in income, benefits, or job stability.

Some skills become outdated quickly; job roles evolve fast. What was safe 5 years ago may not be safe now unless you keep adapting. Also, skill-based hiring is growing — less emphasis on credentials/long tenure and more on what the person *can do now*.

Considering the reduced job security, it has become extremely critical to focus on Financial Freedom and planning ahead of time.

Artificial Intelligence (AI) is transforming the workplace rapidly, automating tasks previously performed by humans and reshaping job markets globally. While AI enhances productivity and innovation, it also presents significant challenges to job security and income stability, making financial Freedom increasingly vital.

AI technologies—like machine learning, robotics, and natural language processing are automating routine, repetitive, and some cognitive tasks. Sectors such as manufacturing, customer service, finance, and even healthcare are experiencing automation-driven shifts. According to recent studies, millions of jobs worldwide face the risk of automation in the coming decades. While new jobs will emerge, many require advanced skills or adaptability.

The transition caused by AI can lead to job displacement, wage stagnation, or changes in career paths. Many workers may face temporary unemployment or need to reskill frequently to remain employable. This economic uncertainty emphasizes the fragility of relying solely on employment income, particularly for younger generations like millennials and Gen Z, who are more exposed to gig economy roles and contract work.

In this changing landscape, **Financial Freedom (FF)** becomes an essential life goal. FF provides a financial safety net, reduces stress related to job insecurity, and offers freedom to make career choices without economic pressure. It encourages disciplined savings, investments, and building multiple income streams.

Surveys show that millennials and Gen Z place comparatively higher importance on Financial Freedom, partly driven by witnessing economic disruptions like AI-driven job changes and the COVID-19 pandemic. They prioritize flexible work, entrepreneurship, and financial literacy to safeguard their futures.

AI's impact on jobs is accelerating uncertainty in employment and income stability. Achieving Financial Freedom empowers individuals to navigate these changes confidently, offering resilience against job disruption. Emphasizing financial literacy, adaptive skills, and proactive planning will be key for individuals and societies to thrive in the AI era.

TCS to axe 12,000 jobs, IT giant's biggest layoff ever

Accenture lays off 11,000 employees, warns more job cuts

Laid-off techies struggle for jobs

Some of the other compelling reasons to prioritize Financial Freedom as a goal are to do with your own well-being and family time, i.e.

- Many traditional jobs come with pressure: long hours, bad bosses, constant deadlines. When you're financially independent, you can walk away from toxic work — and only take on projects you enjoy. Chronic work stress contributes to burnout, poor sleep, and even illness.
- Whether it's family, travel, hobbies, or health, early semi-retirement gives you time back. It's about living life while you're still young and healthy — not waiting until the 60s.
- Having control over your schedule is very powerful vs. earning more money, which increases your accumulation potential.

Key Takeaways

- *Employment scenario is changing faster than you have imagined*
- *Jobs are being redefined or eliminated due to automation and AI*
- *Reduce your dependency and aim for financial freedom*
- *It may not be possible for everyone to forecast the impact on their work stream, and it is much better to prepare yourself considering a worst-case scenario*

The 'Business Case' for Financial Freedom

a. Chasing 'moving goal posts' to 'jumping the treadmill' – A real story

b. Gaining control of your time

c. Changing employment scenario

d. Prepare for the 'Pandemic'

PREPARE FOR THE 'PANDEMIC'

Most of us living in 2025 would equate 'Pandemic' with COVID, but what I mean is much broader. One of the key drivers for a financial freedom journey should be the changing world order and risks much higher than in the past. These risks in the past have erupted in different forms:

- **Great Depression (1929 – 1939):** Most severe economic downturn in modern history, beginning with the Wall Street crash of 1929 and leading to widespread unemployment as well as bank failures globally.
- **Dot-com Bust (2001):** A speculative bubble in internet-related companies that burst, leading to a sharp decline in stock prices and a recession.

  Thousands of start-ups shut down almost overnight. Big companies like Cisco, Intel, Oracle, and HP froze hiring or laid off staff. Estimates suggest that over 200,000 tech workers lost jobs in the U.S. between 2000–2002. Many newly graduated engineers and IT professionals faced unemployment or underemployment for a long time post the bust. Venture capital funding, which had been fuelling aggressive hiring, dried up. Start-ups could no longer afford high salaries or large teams. Recruitment slowed drastically in tech hubs, leading to financial insecurity for many.

- **Global Financial Crisis (2008):** A worldwide banking crisis triggered by the collapse of the U.S. housing market and the subprime mortgage crisis.

  The GFC began in 2007 with the collapse of the U.S. housing bubble and the failure of major financial institutions (like Lehman Brothers in 2008). It led to a global credit crunch, falling demand, and a sharp economic contraction. As businesses lost access to finance and consumers cut spending, unemployment rose sharply.

  The International Labour Organization (ILO) estimated that over 22 million jobs were lost globally between 2008 and 2009. The global unemployment rate jumped from 5.6% in 2007 to 6.2% in 2009. In the U.S., unemployment peaked at 10% in 2009, the highest in decades. In the EU, over 25 million people were unemployed by 2010.

  Long-term unemployment increased — many who lost jobs in 2008 remained unemployed for over a year. GFC led to the rise of part-time, gig, and contract work as companies avoided long-term commitments.
- **COVID-19 (2020):** A global recession caused by the COVID-19 pandemic. It included a sharp stock market crash in February 2020 and led to a global

economic shutdown. Many lost jobs and faced long-term financial insecurity, apart from health issues emanating from the pandemic.

These are just a few examples of global events which lead to significant job losses, recession, and financial capital erosion for many. If you believe these cannot and will not happen in the future, you are being super optimistic. The best way to prepare for such a crisis is to have a financial freedom plan (or may be at least an emergency fund) that helps you if such a crisis were to happen in your lifetime.

Key Takeaways

- *Do reflect on the period of COVID once in a while and try visualising if you would be prepared if the next pandemic (in any form) was to be longer or bigger*
- *Global events can lead to recession and no one can predict the next one so better prepare for one*

World is turning more fragile than ever – Financial Freedom is your insurance against next pandemic & uncertainties of life

Breaking the Pattern: Why 'We' Struggle & Path to Success

a. Lack of Financial Literacy

b. Mindset Shift

c. Waiting for the 'Big Day'

LACK OF FINANCIAL LITERACY

First and the biggest gap is the lack of financial literacy as well as long-term financial planning in India. Most people find personal finance just a good-to-have skill rather than a must-have ability.

One key factor which contributes to the above is the lack of structured financial literacy programs as part of our education system or curriculum – Its high time we realise the importance of making the next generation financially literate. I meet many teenagers and people in their 20s / 30s who don't understand the basics of finance, which is extremely critical for a fulfilling life, in addition to earning ability or skills.

Saving and investing for your future goals is one of the key life skills that everyone should learn, irrespective of their educational background or profession.

As per WEF's study titled '**How to improve outcomes for India's next generation through financial literacy**';

- India continues to face a significant financial literacy gap, with only 27% of Indian adults being financially literate, which is far below the average of 52% in advanced economies.

- While India's Generation Z (approx. 377 million individuals between ages 12 and 27) already accounts for around 43% of India's consumer spending, many are growing up without the essential skills needed to manage money & build financial security.
- In fact, the World Economic Forum's Global Retail Investor Outlook Survey revealed that 51% of Indian individuals seem to be struggling to meet their debts and liabilities, far exceeding the global average of 32%.

Report further underscores that if India's next generation is to thrive economically, we must go beyond looking at financial literacy as an isolated concern and instead acknowledge it as a foundation for better financial outcomes at scale. Without equipping young people with the skills to manage money, credit, and investments, India risks raising a generation vulnerable to debt traps and limited upward mobility.

Second, there are very few conversations around this goal in Indian households, leading to a lack of importance being assigned by mentors/parents/Teachers at a younger age. In fact, even if there are conversations, most of these discussions are around saving, spending and very little around investing – let alone investing based on specific life goals with Financial Freedom as one of the key ones.

Third, the adoption of the Financial Freedom goal as a key part of life goals and then efforts towards this are insufficient. Most individuals find it difficult to visualise the possibility of Financial Freedom in their 20s. The key concern is saving for multiple goals with limited income.

But in reality, Financial Freedom is less about big wins and more about consistent small steps

As Confucius said,

> *"The man who moves a mountain begins by carrying away small stones."*

Financial literacy is not only critical to appreciate the need for financial freedom but even to make basic life decisions like investing, buying a house, risk management by insuring your family (Health as well as Life cover). Most youngsters who start working in their 20s don't understand some of these basics of finance, though they may have high earning ability/skills.

In my own case, despite being a Chartered Accountant who qualified at the age of 23, my level of understanding of financial markets or even the basics of managing your own finances was below average, if not poor. I made some extremely poor decisions in life early on, but have been lucky to have lived through or overcome many of those disasters.

Let me tell you a few basics that I missed as I started my career:

- I bought my first Life Insurance cover (Term Plan) after 9 years of working at the age of 32. Despite the delay, the cover would have been absolutely insufficient if something were to happen to me. All my family's financial goals, like kids' education, housing, etc., were ahead of me, but I completely missed the math behind the cover.
- I had a home loan for the house I lived in and had some savings from a foreign stint in my career, but I became overly conservative and paid off the loan rather than investing in some high-growth assets for some time at least. I would have cleared the loan in 5-7 years, just out of the earnings on the capital, given the stage of life I was in.
- I overinvested in real estate at the start of my career, blocking significant upfront capital (down payment), and diverted my savings towards EMIs, which yielded extremely poor returns in the longer term.

Let me share some embarrassing numbers, but there is a lot of learning hidden in them. In 2013, I was offered a commercial real estate (a small Shop cum office - SCO) in a decent location but without any certainty of success in the market. While I did not understand anything about commercial real estate, the idea of owning an SCO, which can be used tomorrow for your own venture or could be 'let out', fascinated me. I needed to pay about 40% upfront and the rest in instalments, so I liquidated a few stocks that I was holding. 2 of these stocks were good long-term capital goods businesses and are up about 8 times in the last 12 odd years, while the real estate that I invested in hasn't even doubled due to oversupply and multiple other issues. Now, this might be an extreme example, and some people could be lucky with real estate as well, but it is so dependent on timing, right location, future outlook, etc., and the success rate is very low. On the other hand, the stock market in a country like India offers opportunities for a longer term, almost at any time of the year or decade!

Now, some of these are learnings in hindsight, and the idea behind this book, in a way, is not to regret it but rather make sure you don't make some of these mistakes.

Key Takeaways

- *Financial literacy is a must-have skill rather than just a good thing to have*
- *Financial literacy is not only critical to appreciate the need for financial freedom but even to make basic life decisions like investing, risk management, etc.*
- *Without equipping young people with the skills to manage money, credit, and investments, we may risk raising a generation vulnerable to debt traps or even over spending*

Breaking the Pattern: Why 'We' Struggle & Path to Success

a. Lack of Financial Literacy

b. Mindset Shift

c. Waiting for the 'Big Day'

MINDSET SHIFT

Beyond awareness, the other big issue is the mindset or underappreciation of the importance of Financial Freedom in one's journey – Without this change in mindset, one will never put any effort towards these critical life goals.

Financial freedom is often mistaken as a purely mathematical goal — a function of income, savings rate, and returns. In truth, it begins with mindset, not money. The journey toward financial independence is shaped far more by how one thinks about money than by how much one earns.

Most people are conditioned to view money as something to spend rather than something to build with. A mindset change starts with redefining money as a tool for freedom, not just comfort or status. When you start measuring every expense against your long-term independence goal, impulsive consumption will naturally give way to more intentional living.

Financial freedom demands patience. The compounding of wealth — like the compounding of habits — works only with time and consistency. Developing a mindset that values long-term satisfaction over short-term pleasure helps resist lifestyle inflation and peer comparison, both of which quietly erode savings.

Earning more doesn't guarantee freedom; owning productive assets does. A crucial mindset shift is moving from "How can I earn more?" to "How can I make my money work for me?" This shift from active income to passive wealth creation is what separates financially free individuals from high or perpetual earners.

Many avoid investing due to fear — fear of losing money, making mistakes, or entering markets or financial products they don't understand. Changing mindset means accepting the need and then replacing fear with confidence through financial literacy. When you understand risk, you stop fearing it and start managing it.

Comparison-driven spending is one of the biggest roadblocks to financial independence. A healthy mindset focuses on progress, not prestige. **Financial freedom is deeply personal — the ability to choose your time, purpose, and peace — not to outspend others.**

The idea behind mindset shift is that once one understands the importance of financial freedom, one must ACT with full conviction and commitment to achieve the same by a pre-defined age. This will vary based on your starting point, risk tolerance, ability, etc. Let me explain the impact of any delay in appreciation of this with an example:

- Individual A – 25 Years – Single Child – Parents have their own home
- Individual B – 25 Years – Has Siblings – Parents stay in a rented home, or the home is not sufficient to take care of the needs of both the siblings

Now, if you look at the above example, the financial freedom journey could be much faster for Individual A (provided the focus on this goal is clear), as he/she does not have to take care of housing goals, which implies one less goal for saving. Having said that, most individuals would take this as an advantage and end up spending much higher than their peers on 'wants' or 'luxuries' rather than prioritising financial freedom goals.

The ability to achieve financial freedom is more dependent on focus, mindset, and commitment than on your starting point. Therefore, while the timing could be different for the above 2 instances, however its possible for anyone to achieve this.

As Mahatma Gandhi said:

> *"Strength does not come from physical capacity. It comes from an indomitable will."*

Key Takeaways

- *Mindset shift is critical for the FF journey*
- *The journey toward financial independence is shaped far more by how you think about money than by your earnings.*
- *A mindset change starts with redefining money as a tool for freedom, focuses on progress, and not on showing off or displaying wealth*

Breaking the Pattern: Why 'We' Struggle & Path to Success

a. Lack of Financial Literacy

b. Mindset Shift

c. Waiting for the 'Big Day'

WAITING FOR THE 'BIG DAY'

Most people don't start their Financial Freedom journey as they think their cash flow or savings rate is too low for such a long-term and sometimes intimidating or substantial goal. People postpone saving, waiting for a better salary, fewer expenses, or the "perfect" financial moment. But life events rarely stop — there's always a next purchase, celebration, or commitment waiting in line.

Waiting for the perfect day only delays your financial freedom journey.

Just a 5-year delayed start could impact your corpus by half in the end. This seems so simple, but very difficult to appreciate at the beginning of your journey. Let's understand this with some real numbers:

Monthly Investment: INR 10,000 at the expected Rate of Return of 15% p.a.

- Corpus at year 25 if you start right now: ~ 3.3 Crore
- Corpus at year 25 if you start after 5 years: ~ 1.5 Crore

** Estimated values using the Zerodha SIP Calculator available online*

Typical self-doubts or questions most people face as they start saving/investing for their goals are the following:

- I don't have enough savings currently and will do this once I have a better savings rate
- The goal is too far in the future, and I can start anytime later
- Let me focus on the present lifestyle and not worry too much about the future – You only live once (YOLO syndrome)

These are very natural doubts for anyone, but one needs to move beyond them and make a beginning with a view that no amount is small - the more time for your goal, the easier it is to achieve with long-term compounding potential.

Treat saving as a non-negotiable monthly obligation (Save first, Spend later). Set up auto-transfers to mutual funds, SIPs, or recurring deposits, or any other asset of your choice, right after payday. This simple automation removes emotional bias in decision-making and ensures discipline.

The real big day isn't your next bonus or promotion. Rather, it's the day you take control of your future and plan the finances for it. This single decision or mindset shift sets the tone for independence, security, and peace of mind.

Key Takeaways

- *Mindset change and starting small but early for all your long-term goals, including Financial Freedom, would add significant value in the long term.*

Invest time in life skills like Financial Literacy & Let today be your 'Big Day' for a meaningful life of your choice in the future

Journey of 'Freedom of Choice'

- **First things first**

a. How much is 'Enough' – Finding the 'Magic Number'

b. Understand the basics

- **Executing the Plan**

a. Starting the 'Journey' with a Plan

b. Build a strong foundation

c. Asset Classes & Importance of Equity

d. Where & How to 'Start'

e. Asset Allocation & Timing

f. Importance of Gold in your Journey

g. Golden 'Habits'

- **Avoiding the 'disruptors'**
- **Some practical tips – Experience sharing & Perspective**

FIRST THINGS FIRST: HOW MUCH IS ENOUGH – FINDING THE MAGIC NUMBER

First step in the planning process is to calculate your Financial Freedom number i.e., the required corpus post which one can be assumed to be financially free. To get to that number, a few important variables are as follows:

- Your current monthly spend
- How long is the period by which you intend to be financially free
- Lifestyle you would want to maintain post financial freedom

Let's go step-wise and try calculating the same for an average young couple.

Estimate Current Cost of Living: Calculate your monthly spend as a family currently. Here are a few tips to use while doing this:

- Categorise your spending habits into the following buckets, which would generally be sufficient for any working professional / business owner:

- *Baseline*
  - Kitchen and Groceries (Includes Veggies, Milk, Cooking Gas, etc.)
  - House Help / Utilities
  - Rental or Home EMI, as the case may be
  - Transport (EMI, Fuel, Insurance, Servicing, or Shared Transport costs if you rely on the same)
  - Mobile, Broadband & OTT
  - Insurance (Term, Medical)
- *Discretionary*
  - Eating out / Entertainment
  - Travel – Annual vacation, etc. & Misc.

- *Make sure you have considered annual costs like Car Insurance, AMCs, etc., while calculating the above*
- *Don't just guess the expense – Rather, monitor your real costs over at least a 6-12-month window and then take that as a base. Too many people guesstimate this number and end up going completely wrong.*
- *In India, Inflation impact on cost-of-living ranges generally between 4-6%. While planning, one should consider the higher end of Inflation given that some of the cost elements (like medical & higher education) are experiencing much higher inflation – sometimes in excess of 10-12%.*
- Convert the above to an annual number by multiplying monthly costs by 12
- Now, we need to optimise the costs based on certain assumptions, e.g. Housing or mortgage would be done by the time you achieve financial freedom.

- Let's understand this with the help of an example, which would make this calculation easier:

Monthly Costs – Indicative for a young couple in Metro / Large City (Amount in INR thousand)

Cost Element	Current Cost (Per month)	Optimised Cost
Kitchen & Groceries	15k	15k
House Help & Utilities	8k	8k
Rental / Home EMI	50k	Note 1
Transport (EMI, Fuel, Insurance, Servicing, or Shared Transport costs if you rely on the same)	20k	10k Note 2
Mobile, Broadband & OTT	2k	2k
Insurance (Term, Medical) & Medical expenses	10k	10k
Entertainment (Eating out, Travel, Misc.)	20k	20k
Total	**125K**	**65K**

Disclaimer: *This is just an indicative cost to explain a point and will vary based on personal situation/need of the family. If you stay in a smaller city/town, your cost of living could be significantly lower. Idea is to provide a template which can be modified to develop your own calculation.*

Note 1: *Ideally, if you aspire to achieve financial freedom, a house to live in (free of any mortgage obligations) is a* *must-have and hence not considered as a cost post financial freedom. In goal-based investing, this would be taken care of as a separate goal.*

Similarly, a corpus for higher education of kid/s would be separately taken care of as part of the goal-based investing.

Note2: *Car EMI etc. is taken care of as you decide to be financially free, so only running expenses and fuel costs are considered. If you intend to change car every few years, add that as part of the cushion you may want to build as part of the corpus. This applies to all one-time costs that you may be wanting to spend.*

Extrapolate the Current Cost of Living estimate for the future (based on your target age at Financial Freedom)

Now that we have figured out our annual spending (optimised for the future), a simple rule of thumb (considering the inflation in India) is to assume the cost of living would go up 2X every 10-12 years, so if your financial freedom target is 20-25 years away, you should assume 4X of your current living costs (optimized for future) for planning purposes. On the contrary, if your goal is 10-12 years away, then assuming 2X would be a good starting point. More on this mental math or quick calculation in the subsequent section on basics.

Considering the above numbers, one would need about INR 2.6 lac a month (65K * 4) after ~ 25 years from now, factoring in the inflation. Do keep in mind these are starting figures and will need to be re-evaluated as life evolves, so don't stress too much about it. Get to a reasonable estimate and start – that's the goal.

Once we know the spend requirement, the next step is to calculate the total corpus needed to manage the monthly spending.

Corpus needed for Financial Freedom

Now that we have the extrapolated cost of living considering financial freedom post 20-25 years from now, the next step is to estimate the corpus needed for the same at the time of financial freedom.

There are multiple calculators available online (some of which are shared as part of the appendix of this book for you to try), and multiple studies have been done on this subject, which have provided varied results. Let us spend some time on understanding this in some more detail, considering this is one of the most critical elements of the planning process. In the end, I will try providing my directional advice (not a prescription), which one can consider as a starting point (subject to individual circumstances, though).

Most of these rules / calculators are focussed on retirement and hence assume no other income which may be very conservative for people aiming for financial freedom but may still be gainfully employed though could be with lower earning (given the focus will shift towards following your passions / desires rather than just making money) – we will discuss the implication of this on the freedom number at the end of this section as we conclude.

Guiding Rules to calculate your Freedom Corpus

- **The famous 4% Withdrawal Rule (or 25X Corpus Rule) – William Bengen Study of 1994**

The original study behind the 4% rule was conducted by financial advisor William Bengen, which was published in the Journal of Financial Planning in 1994. Mr. Bengen's research concluded that for a retirement of 30 years, a portfolio invested in a 50-50 mix of stocks and bonds could sustain a withdrawal rate of 4% annually, adjusted for inflation, without being depleted, i.e., you need about 25X of your expenses to be financially free.

So, if you go by this rule, you need about 25X of your annual expenses at the time of achieving financial freedom, and you could be sorted.

While I would recommend that you study the whole report (it's a fascinating read which has been simplified to mention 4% rule for ease, and can add a lot of perspective to your freedom journey), but here are a few key points that the study found which are camouflaged behind this over simplified 4% rule:

- His actual figure in the study was 4.15 % withdrawal rate, which he rounded off to 4%
- Assuming a minimum requirement of 30 years of portfolio longevity, a first- year withdrawal of 4 percent, followed by inflation-adjusted withdrawals in subsequent years, should be safe. This essentially means you can start with 4% withdrawal from your total corpus and keep increasing the withdrawal for inflation every subsequent year. (This approach is true for all the methods / guidelines discussed here)
- In no past case has this rule caused a portfolio to be exhausted before 33 years, and in most cases, it will lead to a portfolio life of 50 years or longer. This is the reason 4% is considered the safe withdrawal rate by most people.
- While 4% was considered safe, Mr Bengen also concluded that a very safe rate of initial withdrawal is 3 per cent, i.e., 33X (to the extent history is a guide). This ensures that portfolio longevity is never less than 50 years. This is also true for withdrawal rates as high as approximately 3.5 percent or 29X.
- Rule assumes 50 / 50 allocation to Equities (growth & risk assets) and Bonds (Fixed income safe assets)
- Increasing stock allocation up to 75% can be considered based on one's 'comfort zone', and the same can help in increasing the corpus/wealth over longer periods. Anything more than 75% in stocks/equities could be counterproductive as per the study.

- As per the study, A negative feature of a higher stock allocation is reduced portfolio longevity as a result of a Depression-like event. On the other hand, A major positive is the vastly increased wealth that will accrue under most other scenarios. The balance is tilted in favour of the higher allocation, but it is an individual choice.
- **Update:** Mr Bengen's latest research in 2025 has upped the safe withdrawal rate to 4.7%, which means you only need about 21X of your annual spending as savings to be financially free.

❖ Trinity Study of 1998

Another classic study in the field of financial and retirement planning is the Trinity Study. This study comes out of the article, *"Retirement Spending: Choosing a Sustainable Withdrawal Rate," by Philip L. Cooley, Carl M. Hubbard, and Daniel T. Walz (all professors at Trinity University in Texas),* which appeared in the February 1998 issue of the Journal of the American Association of Individual Investors.

Again, reading the detailed study is recommended, but here are a few key things:

- Trinity Study also found that a 4% withdrawal rate is a reasonable assumption and had a good success rate depending on the mix of equity and debt in one's portfolio.

- In brief, the study concluded the following, apart from many other data points:
  - A 50/50 (Equity/Debt) portfolio with a 3 % withdrawal rate has 100% success rate for a 30-year retirement, while the same with a 4% withdrawal rate drops to 95%.
  - Similarly, A 75/25 (Equity/Debt) portfolio has a 100 % success rate with 3% and 98% success rate with 4%, for a 30-year period
  - Higher allocation of stocks will likely lead to significantly higher terminal value at the end of the 30 years. However, this could also, in some scenarios, increase the failure rates.

❖ Indian Study on Safe Withdrawal Rate (SWR) by Rajan Raju & Ravi Saraogi, CFA

While both the above studies are more based on Western historical data, there is a more recent Indian study that has been done considering the Indian context (specifically inflation & returns from equity in India, which are expected to be higher).

The paper called 'Balancing Acts: Safe Withdrawal Rates in the Indian Context', published by Rajan Raju & Ravi Saraogi, CFA, during January 2024, provides guidance on safe withdrawal rates with the Indian context in mind.

Here are some of the key points of this study:

- The often cited 4% rule is not appropriate in India's context; rather, a range between 3.0% and 3.5% is more appropriate.
- Their analysis reveals that while portfolios with higher equity allocations can potentially increase safe withdrawal rates, they also significantly increase the risk of portfolio failure, particularly for withdrawal rates greater than 3.75%.
- Another highlight of the study is the importance of gold as a diversifying asset, which can mitigate some market-related risks in traditional two-asset class portfolios.
- The relatively short time span of the data, covering just over two decades (2000 to 2023), may not fully encapsulate longer-term economic cycles or market behaviours that could significantly impact retirement portfolio sustainability.
- The key takeaway for investors is to consider moderating their withdrawal expectations, with a target Withdrawal Rate that does not exceed 3.5%, which translates to a corpus of about 30 times expected annual expenses at retirement.
- They have highlighted the importance of regular portfolio reviews and strategic rebalancing, which are crucial to navigate the sequence of return risk and adapt to changing circumstances.
- Study also suggests that beyond a certain point, an increase in equity allocation does not proportionally

increase the SWR due to increased sequence-of-return risks. A balanced and diversified portfolio strategy, combining equities with more stable assets such as fixed deposits and gold, will likely maintain the balance between risk and return.

❖ **Guardrails Theory** *(Suggests a lower Corpus for Financial Freedom)*

Guardrails framework is another approach that has been highlighted or talked about by many researchers, which helps in bringing down the corpus needed, provided one is flexible to adjust the spending patterns based on portfolio performance.

The most well-known guardrails framework was developed by financial planner Jonathan Guyton and computer scientist William Klinger, which is also known as the Guyton-Klinger Approach. The guardrails approach to flexible retirement planning has also been studied by Morningstar.

Essentially, the approach suggests that a higher than 4% withdrawal rate (initial) adjusted for inflation every year can be sustained, provided one is flexible to bring down the spending during years of low portfolio performance, i.e., in the years in which portfolio value has dropped.

While this theory can be attractive for many, as it can bring down the requirement of corpus to as low as 20X (5% withdrawal rate), but adjusting the expenses with this kind of flexibility may not be doable for many. Hence, I haven't considered this approach as part of this section.

Having said that, it's not very difficult. If you can maintain the guardrails and be flexible with your spending, go ahead and adopt this. Enough material is available online that can be referred to, but I am avoiding considering the limitations.

Conclusion

If you consider the above studies, the range of first year withdrawal rates suggested is between 3-4% based on multiple factors I.e. Corpus equivalent to 33X to 25X of annual expenses. As I said, there are some studies (with guardrail approach) which have even suggested a 5% withdrawal as well (i.e., Corpus of 20X of annual expenses) with a fairly good success rate, provided you are flexible to manage your spending based on how your portfolio has done over time. Some of us may want to consider this as an option, but I won't get into that, considering the risks involved, and let's consider the above 3-4% range for now and simplify it in the form of a table with the recommendation to start the Journey:

Safe Withdrawal Rate (%)	Annual Spend Multiple Needed	Remarks
3	~ 33 X	*Safe by most standards* *Possible to leave some inheritance* *Useful in case of longer Freedom years*
3.5	~ 30 X	*Safe by most standards* *Possible to leave some inheritance* *Useful in case of longer Freedom years*
4 ***(Recommended for Planning with tweaks based on Individual Needs over time)***	~ 25 X	*Safe but may need tweaks in case of higher inflation or lower returns* *Might need minor lifestyle adjustments in rare cases*

So, we should start with anywhere between 25X to 30X for planning purposes.

The simplest rule followed by many is called the 25X rule (also called as 4% safe withdrawal rate rule), whereby you multiply the extrapolated annual cost of living number by 25 (i.e., INR 2.6 lac*12*25 = **INR 7.8 Crore**) to get to the corpus needed for financial freedom. This corpus assumes your other needs, like Housing, Child

Education (or marriage goals, if any), and Insurance, are taken care of separately.

To conclude, considering the indicative costs in the example, our corpus requirement for Financial Freedom at the end of ~ 25 years comes out to be INR 7.8 Crore. We will use this number as the base for investing / wealth building for freedom goal as we move ahead.

As I said, some of the latest studies focused on India-specific data suggest a safe withdrawal rate of about 3 to 3.5 percent, making the corpus requirement about 30X, which increases our corpus need in the above example, but I would recommend 25X as a starting point for the following key reasons:

- We are looking at a financial freedom stage and not really a retirement, hence assuming that you would not be able to make some side income through any passion projects or freelancing, may be very conservative
- Financial Freedom does not mean that you stop working forever; it means you have a reasonable cushion to try a few things and decide the future course without worrying about household spending even if you decide to not work any further, etc.
- Some of us might have some inheritance, even if small, which could add to the already planned corpus over time
- If you are flexible to follow the guardrail approach, you may have enough cushion even with a 25X rule.

- You will still have the option of revisiting this as you move ahead hence starting with an average (neither conservative nor aggressive) would make sense

If these numbers still seem high and daunting to begin with, let me try to calm your nerves with some perspective.

- If you assume the freedom target 20 years away and 15% compounding of wealth, you need about 50 Lakh of savings today (lump-sum) to reach this number over 20 years (compounding would make this 16X over 20 years) – More on this in the chapter on 'Understanding the basics.'
- Also, once you factor the increase in income-earning ability over time and look at better investing strategies (e.g. Step up as your income grows), which would make the accumulation of this large-looking number easier – More on this in the subsequent section as we get into implementation of the plan for your freedom journey.

Further, if you are flexible with your discretionary spends, you could even look at ideas to optimise the cost of living, which eventually should help you reduce the need for this corpus.

Ideas to reduce Corpus needed

Lifestyle costs are extremely individualistic and depend on the aspirations of individuals. Variation in lifestyle costs could favourably impact the required corpus by about 20-25%, though any call should be taken after thinking through and understanding one's aspirations. Further, for married couples, it is critical to have an alignment between both partners on this to avoid future conflicts/ issues.

Typically, the following terms define the category of Financial Freedom you would want to achieve:

Type of Financial Freedom	Corpus Needed	Key Points
Lean Financial Freedom	About 20% lower than Baseline	Frugal / Minimalistic Lifestyle Strict Budgeting & spending Discipline
FAT Financial Freedom	Higher than normal	No compromise on lifestyle Higher Travel and Entertainment budgets

Some of the practical ways (though they need a mindset shift), one can look at Lean FI is by relooking at the following life choices:

- *Moving to a Tier II city (or even your hometown if that's an option)* – Most practical way to reduce your need for the overall corpus needed to achieve financial freedom is to look at options of relocating to smaller towns/ cities with good connectivity but much lower cost of living and better lifestyle.

  Typically cost of living in smaller towns is ~20 -40 % lower for the same lifestyle, though one must be mentally prepared to live in a different / smaller city and rebuild social life. While most cities these days generally have all the basic utilities required for a decent lifestyle, it might be important to evaluate the following while looking at the choice of your city:
    - Availability and accessibility of healthcare facilities
    - Support system or social circle in the form of like-minded families
    - Connectivity with bigger towns, considering long term need of your family and kids to travel
    - Possibility of engaging in a remote/hybrid work profile, which would be key to keep one engaged, and it does not turn out to be retirement.
- *Reducing Costs by choosing to live Frugally* – While this is a more difficult path for many, some of us might want to opt for this as well. The most important factor in my view is to avoid the social pressure while choosing this. Once you decide on this path, some of the costs can easily be avoided, provided one is prepared for such a change. Generally, the discretionary spend like

maintaining one's own car vs. relying on call taxis, reducing eating out, etc., can be brought down without much impact on the quality of life, provided one is mentally prepared for the same.

TIP:

- *For the majority, it would be impossible to make a firm choice on whether you would be good with a Lean FI or would prefer a FAT FI. Hence, the plan should always be based on baseline assumptions that can be modified as you go along. Don't stress too much about this in the beginning, as priorities change over time, and your priorities would be very different after 20-25 years – just focus on a baseline plan and focus on making a beginning.*

Start now, Review later

Irrespective of the start point, the journey to financial freedom is going to be long for most people, and given the lifestyle changes and mindset shifts that you will experience over time, it would be almost essential to review the plan every 3-5 years to modify based on revised context. This avoids surprises at the end and keeps your plan current based on your evolved thinking. Do not worry about every small change, but do focus on bigger changes, e.g., additional responsibilities, medical conditions, your aspirations, new passion identification, etc.

Key Takeaways

- *Start with a target corpus based on 25X (or max 30X) rule and keep refining this as your life evolves or as you move ahead in life*
- *Don't stress too much about the right number, as life would evolve and your priorities might change over time. You have a long runway to course correct provided you start early. So, the idea should be just to make a beginning.*
- *Study the Retirement planning research papers in detail once you have the basic financial literacy – you don't have to be an expert to understand this simple math rather you just need to be a bit more conscious about it*

Journey of 'Freedom of Choice'

- **First things first**

a. How much is 'Enough' – Finding the 'Magic Number'
b. Understand the basics

- **Executing the Plan**

a. Starting the 'Journey' with a Plan
b. Build a strong foundation
c. Asset Classes & Importance of Equity
d. Where & How to 'Start'
e. Asset Allocation & Timing
f. Importance of Gold in your Journey
g. Golden 'Habits'

- **Avoiding the 'disruptors'**
- **Some practical tips – Experience sharing & Perspective**

FIRST THINGS FIRST: UNDERSTAND THE BASICS

Now that you know the corpus needed and are ready to start planning your journey, it's important to understand some basics of personal finance, which will help in the corpus creation journey as we move forward. Some of these may be too basic for many, but without these, one may not be fully prepared for a successful journey, so do spend a little bit of time understanding these.

Rule of '72' and '144'

It's a very simple thumb rule, but it is extremely important for basic mental calculations when you are making money decisions.

As per the 'Rule of 72', if you divide 72 by the rate of return that you estimate, you get to know the number of years it will take to double your money. 15% CAGR means your money doubles in ~ 5 years (i.e. 72/15).

It could also be applied to understand the impact of inflation on your savings, i.e., if you divide 72 by the rate of estimated inflation, you can calculate the value of money. 6% inflation means your cost of living doubles in

12 years. Remember the numbers we talked about in the last chapter while extrapolating the corpus needed after 20-25 years.

Similarly, the Rule of '144' is used to calculate the time it would take for your money to quadruple (4X). Simply divide 144 by the rate of return, and you would get the answer in the number of years it would take for your capital to quadruple.

These rules help you do some simple but effective mental calculations.

Impact of Inflation on long term savings

Inflation is the rise in the price level of goods and services over time. It reduces the purchasing power of money, which means the same amount buys less in the future.

In the long run, inflation erodes the value of money, which means that if your money is not growing faster than the rate of inflation in your place/country of residence, you run the risk of reduced buying power of your money. Let's take an example to elaborate this:

Example:

Assume you invest savings of INR 100,000 in a fixed deposit that yields 6% interest per year and the inflation in your country is also 6%. Now, after 12 years, your money would have doubled with this safe fixed deposit, which might seem good. However, owing to inflation in the country, your cost of living would have also doubled to 2,00,000, making the increased corpus of your savings made 12 years ago useless for any additional needs.

In the same example, if your money grows at 12% while the inflation remains at 6%, your capital would have grown in value to 4X while the cost of living would have grown only 2X in the same period.

Inflation reduces Real Returns. Let's understand this a bit more.

Nominal return = what your bank/fund promises;

Real return = Nominal returns *less* Inflation.

Example: FD returns 6%, inflation 6% → Real return = 0%. Your wealth didn't actually grow.

Hence, it's important to look at ways to grow your money at least higher than inflation for any change in your financial position over time. Wealth creation cannot happen if your portfolio is just generating inflation-matching returns.

This brings us to a very important discussion around types of assets.

Growth Assets vs. Safe Assets – Long-term implications

Saving accounts, FDs, and some bonds may feel safe, but can destroy long-term wealth if returns < estimated inflation. Money kept in a savings bank account for a long time loses value as the inflation is much higher than the rate of return in a savings bank account (typically ~3 percent).

Therefore, for long term goals, investing in Growth Assets → Equities, equity mutual funds, and real estate, which have historically delivered higher than inflation returns are essential.

While we will also learn about the ideal mix between growth & safe assets for balanced investing, it's important to invest in growth assets for longer term goals, and safe assets should be used for short-term goals, e.g. Emergency fund generally should be in safe assets (i.e., Fixed Deposits, Liquid Funds) to avoid volatility during times of need.

Inflation is a silent wealth destroyer. Over decades, it can wipe out the value of savings if money is parked only in low-return assets. To preserve and grow wealth, long-term savings must be invested in assets that consistently beat inflation.

What do we mean by growth assets?

Growth Assets are Investments that aim to increase wealth over the long term by delivering higher returns vs. inflation. These assets generally:

- Carry higher short-term volatility, possible losses.
- Historically have delivered12–15%+ returns annually, depending on asset type.

Examples:

- Equities / Stocks (direct shares, equity mutual funds, index funds)
- Real Estate (growth-oriented) (property for appreciation and rental)
- Commodities like gold (to some extent, though more hedge than a growth)
- Start-ups / Private Equity investments

Safe Assets

- Focused on capital protection and stability, with modest returns. Very low or almost zero risk (in stable economies like India).
- Typically yields 3–7% annually and may not beat inflation over the long term.
- Some of them may erode wealth/value due to lower than inflation returns

Examples:

- Fixed Deposits (FDs) / Recurring Deposits (RDs) / Savings Account
- Government Bonds / Treasury Bills
- Public Provident Fund (PPF), EPF, SSY, Traditional endowment/ULIPs plans
- Debt Mutual Funds (short-term/liquid funds)

Let me try to summarise the above for a better understanding:

Comparison Point	Growth Assets	Safe Assets
Goal	Long term wealth creation	Capital safety + liquidity
Returns	High (12–15%)	Low (4–7%)
Volatility (or Risk)	High (market fluctuations) in short/ medium term but reduces with longer horizon	Very low
Time horizon	Long term (10+ years)	Short to medium term (0–5 years)
Inflation protection	Usually beats inflation	Unlikely to beat inflation

While it is easy to explain these asset classes theoretically, the adoption of growth assets needs more work due to fear and lack of understanding amongst the masses.

SEBI conducted an Investor Survey in India during Sep 2025, and some of the key findings clearly highlight the lack of penetration of risk (read growth) assets and hence low growth of capital in the longer term:

- India's investment culture remains deeply risk-averse, with 80% of Indian households prioritizing capital preservation
- Though ~ 63 % household are aware of at least one securities market product
- There is just ~10 % awareness of products like REITs / InvITs / Corporate Bonds, and the highest awareness is of MF/Stocks, which is also at about 50% households
- While the awareness is high for MF/Stocks, the same is not leading to higher penetration based on the below data points:
    - Only 8.5% households have Demat Accounts
    - Overall household penetration of securities market products is still at ~ 9.5%
    - 6.7% penetration of MF/ETF
    - 5.3 % penetration of Stocks
    - Less than 1 % penetration of REITs / InvITs / Corporate Bonds / AIFs

We need to bridge the gap with better awareness and appreciation of the impact of inflation and growth assets on one's financial journey.

Growing wealth with Growth assets & Power of Compounding

Compounding is the process by which your earnings (interest, dividends, or returns) are reinvested to generate additional earnings over time. In simple words:

"Your money starts earning money, and then that money earns more money."

Compounding is often called the 8th wonder of the world (attributed to Einstein). It works best when you combine time + discipline + patience.

Time Multiplier: The longer you stay invested, the faster your wealth grows because returns start generating returns.

Exponential Growth: Growth is slow in the beginning, but after a point, wealth rises sharply like a snowball rolling downhill.

Wealth Creation Without Extra Effort: You don't have to keep adding large sums — patience and discipline allows small sums to grow into large amounts.

TIP:

- *Start Early → Even small amounts grow big if given enough time with the power of compounding.*
- *Stay Invested → Interruptions or withdrawals break the compounding cycle.*

Example to show the impact on Inaction, Patience and early start:

Amount Invested in Year 0 Rate of Return	10 Lakh 15 %
Year 10	40 Lakh
Year 20	1.6 Crore
Year 30	6.4 Crore

Charlie Munger once said

'Wealth crawls in the beginning, walks later before it starts to sprint.'

This one statement (and the table above) is enough for you to understand the importance of compounding and patience in any wealth creation journey.

XIRR vs. CAGR

This is the most basic element one should focus on while evaluating multiple investment options. Other things being equal, the higher the XIRR or CAGR, the better it would be for the long-term compounding of wealth.

Both **XIRR (Extended Internal Rate of Return)** and **CAGR (Compounded Annual Growth Rate)** are popular ways to measure investment returns. While they may sound similar, they are used in different situations and can yield different results depending on the timing and size of investments. Let's understand both:

CAGR – Typically used for Lump Sum Investments

- CAGR measures the **annualized rate of return** on an investment that grows from an initial value to a final value over a specific period.
- Best suited when there is **a single lump-sum investment** and **no intermediate cash flows** (like SIPs or withdrawals).
- Gives a smooth, average annual growth rate assuming the investment grew at a constant rate every year.

Example:

If ₹1,00,000 grows to ₹2,00,000 in 5 years,

CAGR = (2,00,000 / 1,00,000)^(1/5) – 1 = **14.87%**

XIRR – For Multiple Cash Flows (SIPs, Withdrawals, Insurance Products, etc.)

- XIRR calculates the **annualized rate of return** considering **multiple cash inflows and outflows** at irregular intervals.
- Used for SIPs, SWPs, or any investment where money is added or withdrawn over time.
- It accounts for both the **amount and timing** of each transaction.
- Insurance products with multiple inflows and outflows should be evaluated considering XIRR.

Next time your insurance agent pushes for a money-back policy, ask for XIRR on the policy over life and evaluate if it makes sense. Most likely, the agent would avoid this question😊.

Example:

Suppose you invest ₹10,000 every month for 3 years and your investment value is ₹4,50,000 at the end — XIRR will accurately compute the effective annual return based on all cash flows (unlike CAGR, which can't handle multiple dates).

Key Differences

Feature	CAGR	XIRR
Type of Investment	Single lump-sum	Multiple cash flows (like SIP)
Considers Time of Cash Flows	No	Yes
Usefulness	Simplified, smooth annual return	Realistic return considering timing and irregularity
Complexity	Easy to calculate	Requires cash flow data and date-wise entries (Excel or financial calculator)

The 50/30/20 Rule

'50/30/20 rule' is a basic budgeting rule that is extremely simple to implement but has significant advantages in the long run. What really does this mean:

50 – Spend 50 % of the income on 'Needs' defined as essential spends like Rent/ EMI, groceries, utilities, Kids education, etc.

30 - Spend 30 % of the income on 'Wants' defined as Lifestyle spend, which is non-essential but improves quality of life, e.g., dining out, shopping, travel, movies, hobbies, etc.

20 – Save 20 % of the income and invest towards your long-term goals, i.e., emergency fund, Freedom contributions, mutual funds, SIPs, loan repayments, long-term goals (kids' education, home down payment)

While this is the general guidance, however, here is what I think is essential for people aiming for Financial Freedom and goes a long way once you start practicing. For Financial Freedom enthusiasts, just flip the 30/20 to 30% on savings and 20% of wants; this small change can contribute towards the goal of Financial Freedom in the long run.

As your income grows, increase the savings rate higher than the spending on Needs & Wants. As a thumb-rule, your saving rate should reach about 40-50% as your income grows, provided you avoid lifestyle creep. While we will discuss this in more detail in subsequent sections, in brief, this is essentially making sure that your wants don't continue increasing with every income increase. The idea is not that you don't make any changes to your lifestyle as you earn more, but the point is it should not be proportionate to the increase in income, and some part of the increased earnings should enhance the savings rate. If you are really passionate about freedom of choice, i.e., Financial Freedom.

Let us understand this point with a relatable real-life example:

- X has been thinking of upgrading his car due to the expected increase in his income
- His/her Income increases by 25,000 / month due to a promotion.
- His need for the new car can be managed with an EMI of ~ 15-18k / month
- Due to increased income, he ends up buying a car with 25,000/month EMI. The down payment is managed through the exchange of the old car.
- He could have easily bought an upgraded car with about 15-18K EMI and increased his saving rate by 5-7K due to this change, but he chose to spend the whole increase on a car, which is clearly part of 'Wants'.

Such decisions make an impact on the financial freedom corpus in the longer term and must be evaluated appropriately if you value freedom.

TIP:

- *Track your expenses to ensure you are not making significant deviations from the above and make necessary changes if deviations are observed.*
- *Use one-time bonuses, etc., to make a larger contribution (bullet) to your FI corpus. Over time, this adds up and can help you achieve this faster.*

One of the ways you could implement this is by tracking your expenses regularly, which is often under-appreciated or even some may think it's too complicated. Let me tell you a very simple and effective way through multiple apps that you can use to track expenses:

App	Platform(s)	Use Case	Remarks
ET Money	Android, iOS	Popular in India, connects via SMS to auto-track expenses & categorize	Good for Indian users
Money Manager Expense & Budget (Realbyte)	Android, iOS	Clean interface, supports multiple currencies, category breakdowns, calendar view, etc.	Good for categorization
Mint (by Intuit)	Web, Mobile	Very popular globally — aggregates all accounts, tracks expenses, budgets, gives insights & alerts	Works better in countries where bank connection is supported
Spending Tracker – Budget App	Android, iOS	Tracking of expenses in multiple categories	Extremely easy to use

I personally have been using Spending Tracker – Budget App' on iOS and find this extremely helpful to know my spend pattern. I find this very user friendly and its extremely easy to populate your expenses on the go. I wish I had something like this during my initial saving days to tell me the blind spots in my spending patterns.

Key Takeaways

- *Learn about growth assets, CAGR, XIRR and some of the basic finance terms which help you evaluate your investments*
- *These are terms which are as relevant for you as they are for any financial expert*
- *Treat these as life skills and build knowledge of these over time*

Investing your time in gaining financial knowledge or literacy will yield the best return over time.

Journey of 'Freedom of Choice'

❖ **First things first**

a. How much is 'Enough' – Finding the 'Magic Number'
b. Understand the basics

❖ **Executing the Plan**

a. Starting the 'Journey' with a Plan
b. Build a strong foundation
c. Asset Classes & Importance of Equity
d. Where & How to 'Start'
e. Asset Allocation & Timing
f. Importance of Gold in your Journey
g. Golden 'Habits'

❖ **Avoiding the 'disruptors'**

❖ **Some practical tips – Experience sharing & Perspective**

EXECUTING THE PLAN: STARTING THE 'JOURNEY' WITH A PLAN

Once you have clarity around the magic number (read financial freedom number) and understand some basics, it is fairly easy to calculate the amount you need to set aside to reach your goal using any of the online calculators.

To avoid complexity, let us carry forward the corpus calculated in the previous section on calculating your freedom number, i.e., you need about ~ 7.8 Crore at the end of 25 years. If I use any of the MF SIP calculators available online on multiple platforms, it gives me a consistent monthly investment of 24,000 needed for 25 years to reach this goal.

Now, this might sound high to many of us, considering that at the beginning of a career, there are multiple priorities one is trying to fund. The idea is not to get disheartened, if you are unable to reach this saving number for this specific goal in the beginning, rather look for alternatives, e.g. Step up investing.

If you consider the same target number but believe you can step up your investment by 10% annually (fairly practical with an increase in income), you could start with about half of this, i.e., INR 12000, and still reach your end goal.

The other option could be bullet investments during bonus months, which again reduces the monthly investment needed. Let's assume you have 10 lakhs at the start, which is invested in a growth asset like equity, and you could hold this for 25 years. This will yield about 3.2 Crore, assuming 15% rate of return, and your SIP needs for the balance out of 7.8 Crore comes down to ~ 14,000.

This is just an example to emphasise the point that just try creating a plan (even if in your mind) and start with whatever you can. The idea of the plan is to have a conscious and thought-through direction rather than worry about the number in the beginning.

Having said that, it would help to have a Plan that is specific for a point in time and should focus on the following at a minimum:

- Define your vision for financial freedom with the following:
  - Lifestyle you would want to maintain
  - How much of an adjustment would you be willing to make to your current lifestyle, if applicable?
  - The freedom number required to achieve the same

- Assess the Current State
    - List all assets (savings, property, investments) and Liabilities (debt, loans)
    - Calculate current net worth = assets - liabilities.
    - Have you taken care of basics like health/Insurance, Emergency fund, etc.?
- How much would you be able to set aside for this goal on a monthly basis?
- Are you financially aware enough to decide the instruments to use for investing?
- Would you need the help of an advisor?

Try to run through the plan together with your partner and make amendments wherever required, but ensure there is complete alignment on assumptions and the forward path.

Let me make one last point - none of your financial freedom plans are final till you reach the goal. Therefore, it's critical to review the plan and assumptions every 3-5 years based on changes to your lifestyles, expectations, health situation, etc. There are too many variables, and once you start to experience life, aspirations change, and goals keep getting clearer, and hence the review process.

The plan is meant to give you direction and a starting point, but should not bind you forever. Keep some flexibility and make changes as life evolves.

You don't want to end up reaching the wrong goal post based on a static plan.

Key Takeaways

- *Have a plan, even an imperfect one, and just start.*
- *Review every 3-5 years as you evolve.*

Journey of 'Freedom of Choice'

- **First things first**

a. How much is 'Enough' – Finding the 'Magic Number'

b. Understand the basics

- **Executing the Plan**

a. Starting the 'Journey' with a Plan

b. Build a strong foundation

c. Asset Classes & Importance of Equity

d. Where & How to 'Start'

e. Asset Allocation & Timing

f. Importance of Gold in your Journey

g. Golden 'Habits'

- **Avoiding the 'disruptors'**
- **Some practical tips – Experience sharing & Perspective**

EXECUTING THE PLAN: BUILD A STRONG FOUNDATION

The following steps in the early years would go a long way in building a strong foundation for Financial Freedom journey. Many of them may seem small, but they are very significant in making your journey smoother as you go along. Timely action on these areas would be key to ensuring you stay on course on your journey towards financial freedom.

Build an Emergency Fund

An emergency fund is highly recommended as you start working, though the quantum can vary depending upon your financial status and risk tolerance. Let me first define an emergency fund in this context:

Emergency fund is supposed to cover all essential costs (Needs), i.e., rent/mortgage, food, utilities, transport, insurance, loan EMIs, and basic healthcare in case of an emergency, e.g. Job loss / Income loss.

TIP:

- *Never include luxuries or vacations in an emergency fund, which might make this bloated unnecessarily.*

Basic purpose of an emergency fund is to cover **unexpected expenses or income loss**, so you don't need to take loans or **sell investments**. Sell investments is the key here as this could derail your goal-based investing / journey. Hence, this is foundational preparation in our journey towards Financial Freedom and must not be ignored for a robust outcome. I must admit, I did not build an emergency fund at the beginning of my career and have experienced the negative impact it can have on your financials. I kept withdrawing money from my long-term investments for short term needs and it derailed my overall journey.

Typically, as a rule of thumb, I would recommend the following based on experience:

Category	Job Risk	Need
Both Working	High Risk of Job loss	3-6 Months
Both Working	Low to Moderate risk of Job loss	3 Months
Single Working	High Risk of Job loss	9-12 Months
Single Working	Low to Moderate risk of Job loss	3-6 Months

To begin with, most people other than some high-risk professions where the chances of lay-offs are higher (to be assessed based on market conditions, skill set etc.) should be good with about 3-6 months of emergency fund.

What to do: Start with 3 months in case of both working and 6 months in case of single working. This could be enhanced as we go along but for initial career years, it should be fine to have 3-6 months of funds.

An emergency fund is your financial shock absorber and should never be used for vacations, shopping or any other luxuries.

The following is non-negotiable in case of an emergency fund:

- *Safety:* Fund needs to be away from volatility as you cannot time the need for this i.e. an emergency.
- *Liquidity:* You should be able to liquidate them within a 24 to 48 hours.

Therefore, Emergency funds need to be invested in safe assets like Fixed Deposits or Short to medium duration high rated Debt funds.

Get a Term Life Insurance / Cover

Term life insurance is a pure protection plan which provides a lumpsum to your family in case of untimely death or disability of the earning member.

Again, this is one of the most important things when you start your Financial Freedom journey. While as a rule of thumb, Financial planners recommend 10-15X of your annual income but I would recommend that you figure out a number based on following factors:

- *Both working and low dependence on any single member*: While both should take a Life cover however the amount could be lesser compared to the thumb rule
- *Both working and high dependence on one of the members*: While both should take a Life cover, the amount of cover for the higher earning member should be larger.
- *Single working:* Life cover should be for the earning member.

While calculating the required cover, make sure you factor in an amount sufficient to provide for recurring running costs (arising out of loss of the earning individual), add any pending liabilities (Home loan), and future obligations (Kids' higher education) before you arrive at the insurance coverage needed.

In my own view, about 25 times annual spending (not income) plus pending liabilities (Home loan) and future obligations (Kids higher education) should be good in most situations. If this seems higher, you could look at staggering it by starting with a smaller cover initially and increasing it as you go along. While this would be similar to the 10 – 15X of income thumb rule in the beginning, assuming about 50-60 percent costs, but could turn out to be much lower once your income levels grow without an equal increase in the cost of living. Therefore, I prefer the linkage with the cost of living rather than Income.

The premium for a term life is significantly lower if you start early and while you are in good health. As a thumb rule, the premium for coverage doubles every 8-10 years if you delay taking the term cover, i.e., Term life cover of ~ 1 Crore for a 20-year healthy individual is ~ INR 10,000 / year, while for the same cover for a 30-year healthy individual, it could cost ~ INR 20000 / year

TIP:

- *Term life insurance needs should be re-assessed every 3-5 years based on family needs, lifestyle costs, and obligations, if any.*
- *Mixing investment and insurance is never a great idea, and one should prefer a pure term plan for insurance needs. Bankers and insurance agents generally try to sell you Insurance cum investment plans, which need to be avoided in most cases.*

What to do: Start with a cover of 20X of your annual spend plus any pending liabilities, and re-assess every 3-5 years, and make suitable adjustments by increasing or reducing the coverage.

Medical Insurance

Medical Insurance is a must-have to ensure you are covered for medical emergencies, and the same does not impact your savings/investments. It is especially important for people with dependent families, including parents.

One of the most prevalent practices for working professionals is to rely completely on the medical coverage provided by their employers, which has multiple limitations:

1. Coverage ends the moment you leave/lose your job or switch employers with a gap. The gap between one job and the other remains uncovered and could lead to significantly high costs in case of any emergency.
2. Coverage in case of corporate policies is generally low (typically ₹3–5 lakh), which may be insufficient today

Therefore, it's always recommended to have your personal cover, which comes with the following advantages:

1. Stays with you, irrespective of job changes. Covers the gap, if any, in employment.
2. You can have higher coverage, and in case of a large claim, you can first use your employer's cover, and then your personal cover (through top-up policies).

TIP:

- *Best to include your parents as part of your Corporate Insurance plan, even if the option is with some co-payment. This will generally turn out to be cheaper in most cases.*
- *Have a base cover and a top-up cover to save costs. Top-up covers are almost 1/10th of the cost and can provide much more extensive coverage. Top-up covers can be used once the base amount defined in the top-up policy is used.*

Key Takeaways

- *Build an emergency cover as per your needs – typically 3-6 months of expenses, including EMIs, should be good in most cases*
- *Go for a pure term life cover and a sufficient medical cover early on (Top-up covers could be considered to reduce the cost of the cover)*

Journey of 'Freedom of Choice'

- **First things first**

a. How much is 'Enough' – Finding the 'Magic Number'
b. Understand the basics

- **Executing the Plan**

a. Starting the 'Journey' with a Plan
b. Build a strong foundation
c. Asset Classes & Importance of Equity
d. Where & How to 'Start'
e. Asset Allocation & Timing
f. Importance of Gold in your Journey
g. Golden 'Habits'

- **Avoiding the 'disruptors'**
- **Some practical tips – Experience sharing & Perspective**

EXECUTING THE PLAN: ASSET CLASSES & IMPORTANCE OF EQUITY

While execution of the plan for everyone would be different depending on personal preferences, lifestyle, and understanding of various long-term saving instruments, let us try understanding various available asset classes and their respective advantages or disadvantages specifically for a Financial Freedom goal. In the end, we will talk about a practical step-by-step plan to reach the end goal.

Investing journey for long-term goals like financial freedom will go through multiple cycles and is prone to derailment unless supported by experts/professionals. Therefore, while we will draw a broad plan, but its highly recommended to work with a financial advisor before you start to execute the same.

Let's start with the basic understanding. If you were to achieve financial freedom through financial savings or passive income, there are 3 distinct asset classes one could look at:

A. Building a Fixed Income Portfolio

B. Investing in market-linked securities, i.e., the Stock Market

C. Building rental income through real estate (plus the appreciation advantage)

All of them come with different levels of complexity, ease, and success rate, and we will talk about all 3 of them. In the end, we will discuss the preferred option for most.

There is another way to achieve financial freedom, which is not through savings but rather through creating alternate income Streams – YouTube, Online Training Programs, etc. Of late, many have found success in this as well, but it's not for everyone. You may not even know your Ikigai, so better to prepare with finances and then explore something that you would love doing.

Let us try to do a simple comparison of these asset classes based on a few important parameters:

Asset Class	Pros	Cons
Fixed Income	• Predictable and fixed returns • Almost zero risk of capital loss	Generally, does not beat inflation

Real Estate	• Appreciation • Inflation-adjusted Rental yield – Passive Income	• Illiquid - Does not allow Partial exit/ withdrawal • High investment needed • Volatility & low rental yield in India • Maintenance costs • Legal & regulatory issues • Builder / Project Delays
Equity	• Growth Asset providing inflation-beating returns in the long run • High Liquidity	High volatility in the short to medium term

In the Indian context, the best asset class considering the above pros and cons to build long-term wealth for any particular goal is equity, with the biggest advantage being long-term inflation-beating returns, high liquidity, and low risk of capital over a longer time horizon (considering the growth rates of the expected economy for the next couple of decades). Not to say wealth cannot be created with Real estate, but given the higher capital needs and lack of reliable or low-risk options in India, very few people can succeed with this asset class. Having said that, it is possible to build rental income over time, which could help you achieve financial freedom.

I personally find equity markets a far superior choice for longer-term wealth and liquidity, considering the pros, and hence would focus on the next few sections in trying to convince the reader with some data points. This genesis also comes from my personal experience of having tried both real estate and equity. In fact, if I had not tried real estate, I would have achieved financial freedom at least 5-7 years in advance.

Importance of Equity in the current context

Investing in equity essentially means investing in the Stock market through mutual funds or building a portfolio of direct stocks through your own research. Before we get into what could be suitable for most, let's understand some modes through which one can participate in equity markets.

Various Ways to Invest in Equity

Equity investing represents ownership in a company and offers the potential for higher long-term returns compared to traditional fixed-income investments. By participating in the growth of businesses, investors benefit from capital appreciation, dividends, and compounding. In India, there are multiple avenues to invest in equities — ranging from simple mutual funds to customized portfolio management services to direct stocks. The right route depends on an individual's financial goals, knowledge, and risk appetite, and for most Mutual Funds, could offer a reasonable balance.

A. Direct Equity (Stocks)

Investing directly in shares of listed companies gives investors the purest exposure to equity markets. Shares are purchased and held in a Demat account, and transactions are executed via a trading account on stock exchanges like the NSE or BSE.

Advantages:

- Full control over stock selection, portfolio composition, and timing.
- Potential for superior returns through well-researched company selection.
- Eligibility for dividends and corporate actions (bonus, rights, splits).

Key considerations:

- Requires full understanding of business fundamentals, valuations & market cycles.
- High volatility and emotional decision-making can affect returns.
- Best suited for financially savvy investors willing to actively monitor and manage their portfolios.

B. Equity Mutual Funds

Equity mutual funds pool money from multiple investors and allocate it across a diversified portfolio of stocks, managed by professional fund managers. They are ideal for those seeking exposure to equities without the need for active stock picking. The typical cost of a mutual fund ranges between 0.5% to 1.5%, depending on the type and category. So, you get the services of a professional fund manager at a fraction of the cost, which is great for most investors.

There are multiple types of funds that one can choose from – some of which are:

- **Large-Cap Funds:** Invest in well-established, blue-chip companies offering stability.
- **Mid- and Small-Cap Funds**: Target smaller, faster-growing companies with higher risk and reward.
- **Flexi-Cap or Multi-Cap Funds**: Dynamically invest across large, mid, and small companies.
- **Index Funds and Exchange-Traded Funds (ETFs)**: These are passive investment vehicles designed to replicate the performance of a specific market index, such as the Nifty 50, Sensex, or Nifty Next 50. They do not rely on active fund management but aim to mirror the index's returns. Low-cost structure (expense ratios often <0.5%).
- **Thematic and Sectoral Funds**: These funds invest in specific themes (e.g., ESG, Make in India, digital

economy) or sectors (e.g., banking, IT, pharma). They are more concentrated and cyclical than diversified funds. High concentration risk — poor performance of the chosen sector/theme impacts the entire fund.

Advantages:

- Professional management and diversification at a marginal fee.
- Convenient through Systematic Investment Plans (SIPs) starting as low as ₹500.

C. Portfolio Management Services (PMS)

PMS provides customized equity portfolio management to high-net-worth individuals (HNIs), typically requiring a minimum investment of ₹50 lakh (as per SEBI norms). A PMS manager constructs and actively manages a personalized portfolio aligned with the investor's goals, risk profile, and preferences.

Types of PMS:

Discretionary PMS: The portfolio manager takes buy/sell decisions on behalf of the investor.

Non-Discretionary PMS: The investor approves transactions recommended by the manager.

Advisory PMS: Manager only advises; execution remains with the investor.

Advantages:

- Tailored strategy and high transparency (individual stocks held in the investor's name).
- Professional, research-driven portfolio construction.
- Flexibility to adjust positions, sectoral exposure, and cash holdings.

Key Considerations:

- Higher costs (management + performance fees).
- Concentrated portfolios may lead to higher volatility.
- Best suited for investors with long-term horizons and high-risk tolerance.

D. International Equity

Investors can diversify geographically through international mutual funds, global ETFs, or select PMS platforms offering access to U.S., European, or Asian equities. Exposure to global leaders like Apple, Microsoft, or Nestlé helps balance domestic market concentration.

Advantages:

- Diversification across economies, sectors, and currencies.
- Participation in global innovation and consumption growth trends.

Key Considerations:

- Currency fluctuations and foreign market risks.
- Tax treatment differs from domestic equity funds.

Equity investing is central to long-term wealth creation and financial freedom. Each route — from mutual funds to PMS to Direct equity- offers a unique balance of control, effort, and expertise. The right approach depends on your time horizon, risk capacity, financial goals, and involvement level.

Regardless of the path chosen, success in equities ultimately comes from discipline, diversification, and staying invested through market cycles. **For most people, Mutual Funds offer a reasonable balance and would offer a good starting point.**

Assuming you take the mutual fund route, given the risks involved in stock selection, it's best to look at a monthly SIP, which is the simplest for most people.

As we understood in the basics, Equities as a class is a growth asset which if used effectively helps you create wealth and also beat inflation over a long period of time. Before we get into the pros and cons of equity investing for the financial freedom goal, let us understand some historical data about Indian Equities and what lies ahead for us to appreciate this as an asset class.

Historically, Indian equities have given inflation-beating returns over longer holding periods (i.e., at least 10+ years). People who have remained invested in equity over decades have accumulated wealth, and the ones who have looked at the stock market for short-term gains have generally lost wealth. Let us look at a simple table for various indices as of Oct 2025 and look at the returns:

	Annualized Returns			
Symbol	**1Yr**	**3Yr**	**5Yr**	**10Yr**
Nifty 50	2.42	14.93	17.65	13.32
Nifty Next 50	-7.89	18.4	21.15	14.37
Nifty 100	0.59	15.11	18.01	13.43
Nifty 200	0.52	16.41	19.44	13.96
Nifty 500	-0.1	17.1	20.31	14.34

If you look at the above chart, you would realise that while the 1 year returns have been low to negative, any period above 3, the indexes have given returns averaging 13-15%, which beats the inflation in the country by a significant margin.

Having said that, equities do come with higher volatility, and holding them for a longer period of time is not easy for most individuals, given the negative cycles it generally goes through. Here is some data to show you some of the worst crashes in the market.

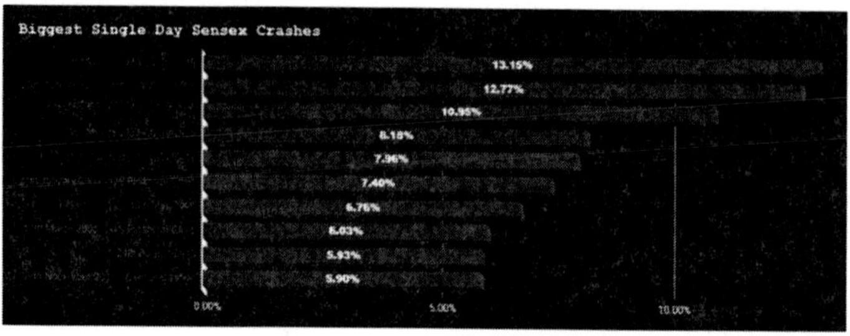

Source: Tradesbrain

Basically, if you were invested in the markets during any of these phases, you could be looking at a 6-13 % drop in a single day, and if you stayed invested throughout the downturn, you could be looking at an overall drop of even 50%, which not many can withstand mentally and emotionally. Let us look at the nearest market fall during the 2020 COVID outbreak:

Date	Nifty 50 Index	% Change
1 Jan 20	12182	
23 Mar 20	7610	38% Drop
31 Dec 20	13982	84% Jump

Such a steep fall in the value of your financial holdings is not easy to handle for any individual – especially when you see your invested capital dropping by 40% within a 3-month window. Now, the above is index-level data, and some of the small-cap funds dropped more than 50% in the same period. My own portfolio was down by about 40%+ during this period.

On the contrary, people who dared to deploy capital at the bottom (easier said than done), would have gained 70-80 % within 9 months. It's the easiest to discuss these extreme falls on paper and almost catastrophic to watch your investment values dip. The tendency to pull out of the market is extremely strong during such downturns.

That brings us to the biggest con of equity investing, i.e. Volatility which isn't easy to handle.

> *Morgan Housel describes volatility as the necessary "price of admission" or "fee" for achieving superior long-term returns.*

While the historical returns of Indian stock markets have been reasonably strong, the future looks even brighter. The next 2 decades could be transformational for India as an economy, given the changes expected. Let's try to forecast the future based on trends and some studies.

- India's per capita income is expected to rise to USD 26000 (India@2047 published in 2022 by PWC), which is approximately 10 times vs. the current per capita income
- By 2030, India is set to become the world's third-largest economy with a projected GDP of $7.3 trillion from the current number of ~ $4 trillion

- India's GDP growth is projected at about 6.5% vs the global GDP growth of ~3%
- India currently contributes about 18% to the world GDP growth
- India has over 800 million people below 35 years — the largest youth population in the world. The demographic dividend window is expected to remain open till 2045, giving India about two decades to harness this advantage

If you look at the data above and some of the other arguments, you should have almost zero doubt on the ability of Indian businesses to grow and hence generate higher than inflation returns for the stocks.

Trading vs. Investing

Investing is about wealth creation over time by participating in the growth of quality businesses through the equity market, whereas trading is about profiting from short-term price movements in stock prices on the exchange.

Investing focuses on **owning quality companies** and holding them through market cycles to benefit from business growth, dividends, and compounding returns. Successful investors emphasize:

- **Long-term perspective:** Staying invested through volatility.

- **Research and fundamentals:** Studying balance sheets, management, and industry trends.
- **Power of compounding:** Allowing returns to grow exponentially over time.
- **Diversification:** Reducing risk by spreading across sectors and market caps.

On the other hand, Trading involves frequent buying and selling of securities to capitalize on short-term market momentum. Traders use technical charts, indicators (like RSI, MACD, and moving averages), and price action to identify entry and exit points.

Trading demands **constant monitoring, emotional control, and risk management** (like stop-loss orders). While it can generate faster returns, the probability of consistent long-term success is relatively low for most individuals, and Trading is generally found to be high risk, and one could lose capital in adverse market movements.

Investing with a long-term horizon and patience during downturns has rewarded investors over the long term and is the best strategy for most. In my personal view, people with financial freedom aspirations should never look at trading as an option, given the potential of capital loss.

Warren Buffett aptly said:

> *"The stock market is a device for transferring money from the impatient to the patient."*

Key Takeaways

- *Equity Mutual Funds could be suitable for most people to build wealth over time*
- *India is at the cusp of a transformational phase, and the next couple of decades definitely hold a lot of potential and seem very encouraging considering the growth expected in per capita income as well as GDP*
- *Volatility is almost given during a long-term equity investment journey, and one should be prepared for the same to avoid exiting the markets in a downward cycle like the COVID period.*
- *Capitalise on market falls to build equity exposure if you have longer horizon*

Journey of 'Freedom of Choice'

- **First things first**

a. How much is 'Enough' – Finding the 'Magic Number'
b. Understand the basics

- **Executing the Plan**

a. Starting the 'Journey' with a Plan
b. Build a strong foundation
c. Asset Classes & Importance of Equity
d. Where & How to 'Start'
e. Asset Allocation & Timing
f. Importance of Gold in your Journey
g. Golden 'Habits'

- **Avoiding the 'disruptors'**
- **Some practical tips – Experience sharing & Perspective**

EXECUTING THE PLAN: WHERE & HOW TO 'START'

I have seen too many people stressing about returns and trying to optimise their investment based on the recency bias. As I write this, the ongoing flavour is Gold and Silver, given the returns over the last couple of years. It's almost impossible for a normal individual investor to figure out the best-performing asset class and chase returns in the beginning.

As you make a beginning and start investing for financial freedom, don't worry about asset allocation or chasing returns, and just begin with about 2-3 good mutual fund schemes. There are far too many categories to confuse any new investor, and here is generic and simplistic advice (assuming you don't want to use a professional investment advisor, which is highly recommended to assess your risk tolerance as well as behaviour).

Investor Type	Basic Traits	Fund Choice (Equal Split)
Aggressive	Can handle volatility with ease	1 Flexicap, 1 Small Cap, 1 Mid Cap

Moderate	Can handle volatility but will panic a bit	1 Flexicap, 1 Mid Cap, 1 Large Cap
Conservative	Can's handle volatility	1 Flexicap, 1 Large Cap

While you should look at the best performing funds, the size of the AMC, and the Fund Manager's track record, don't try to chase the maximum returns. There are cycles every fund goes through, and returns vary in cycles – till the time the fund and the manager have a good track record, there is no point getting bogged down by short term drop in the returns of the specific fund you picked vs. benchmarks.

As you start, it's more important to be disciplined about consistency than chasing returns. In the longer term, time in the market pays the maximum dividend rather than timing the market.

For absolute beginners who have a longer horizon and want to keep it extremely simple, even index investing is a great option.

Index investing is a passive strategy that involves buying and holding a portfolio of securities that match a market index, such as the NSE Nifty 50. By doing so, investors aim to match the performance of the index rather than trying to outperform the market through active stock picking. Index funds are most commonly used to practice this strategy. These funds pool money from many investors to invest in all the stocks or bonds that make up a particular index, in the same proportions as the index itself.

An index fund's performance is directly tied to the index it tracks. If the overall market goes up, the index fund's value will increase. Conversely, if the market declines, the fund's value will also fall.

Some advantages of index investing:

Low cost: Because index funds are passively managed, they have much lower operating costs and expense ratios than actively managed funds. This means more of your investment returns stay in your pocket.

Simplicity and transparency: Index investing is easy to understand, making it a good option for beginners. Since the fund simply mirrors a publicly known index, you always know exactly which securities you own.

Long-term performance: Historically, many actively managed funds fail to consistently outperform their benchmark index over the long term, especially after accounting for higher fees. Index funds offer consistent, market-average returns over extended periods.

On the other hand, one of the downsides of index investing is that it would give you only average returns over time. By definition, an index fund can only match the average market return. It cannot beat the market or benchmarks. For some investors, this may feel like a missed opportunity to generate higher returns.

Generally, Index investing is more suited for mature markets and may not be ideal for a country like India, which is going through a transformational phase and opportunities to create alpha (higher than index return) are much higher provided you rely on experts.

Index investing is a "buy and hold" strategy designed for long-term growth. Stick with your plan, even through periods of market volatility if you want to create wealth. Just for reference, BSE Sensex has given ~ 15% CAGR since inception, which is about 45 years (Starting in 1979).

While everyone should take a call based on their personal preference, here is some perspective with data:

Amount Invested	Value at 20 Years (CAGR@12%)	Value at 20 Years (CAGR@ 15%)	Value at 20 Years (CAGR@ 18%)	Value at 20 Years (CAGR@ 20%)
1 Lakh	9.64 Lakh	16.36 Lakh	27.39 Lakh	38.33 Lakh

If you look at the table above, a 5% higher return compared to the index has resulted in almost 2.5 times the corpus over 20 years. There are a few small-cap or even flexi-cap fund which have yielded that kind of a return in the longer term (at least in the past, though that is no guarantec of future performance).

Considering the above, for an above-average Indian investor with an aggressive risk profile, investing in well-managed active funds (flexi cap or mid/small cap) could be beneficial in the long run, provided one can handle the volatility during the journey.

Leveraging the magic of Step-up investing

As I said, while the amount required for financial freedom might seem daunting at first, it is absolutely possible to achieve the same with consistent investing and some practical perspective.

Based on my practical experience of 25+ years, investing or saving is never linear. The amount that you can save/invest goes up with time if you manage to keep your lifestyle enhancement in check and don't end up buying a bigger car or renovating/upgrading your house every time your salary goes up.

Let me show you the magic of step-up investing, which is absolutely possible to achieve with a bit of discipline and planning.

Scenario 1

Investment / Month	Rate of Return	Tenure	Amount Invested	Accumulated Capital
12,000	15%	25 years / 300 Months	36 Lakh	3.95 Crore

Scenario 2 – Step-up Investing

Investment / Month	Rate of Return	Tenure	Amount Invested	Accumulated Capital
12,000 + 10% step up yearly	15%	25 years / 300 Months	1.42 Crore	7.9 Crore

Scenario 3 – Both working and investing

Investment / Month	Rate of Return	Tenure	Amount Invested	Accumulated Capital
15000 + 10% step up yearly	15%	25 years / 300 Months	1.77 Crore	9.9 Crore

* *Used Zerodha SIP and Step-up calculator for the above*

Scenario 2 assumes that your disposable income goes up as you age, provided you don't increase your lifestyle at the same pace as your increase in income. While we will discuss this in detail in subsequent sections as to how lifestyle creep can derail your financial freedom plans, generally, at a young age, most people underestimate their ability to increase their income, provided you are skilled.

As a thumb rule, if you are working in a decent skill-based role, your salary doubles every 5-6 years. This could be even more for skills which are in demand, and you could potentially look at changing jobs every 3-5 years. Skill-based employment and pay based on skills rather than background would continue to go up in an economy that is growing. Therefore, if you could continue to enhance your skills (technical as well as softer), the growth in earning ability is almost guaranteed, with a lack of skilled talent around. So, let us assume your salary or earning ability goes up every 5-6 years, and try to push more savings towards the financial freedom goal, which could make the journey much easier.

Importance of Habits & the First ₹1 Crore in an Investing Journey

In every investor's wealth-creation journey, the **first ₹1 crore** holds a special significance. It's not just a financial milestone — it's a psychological and mathematical turning point that transforms how wealth grows and how investors think. Building the first crore takes the most time, effort, and discipline, but once achieved, it sets the foundation for **compounding to truly accelerate.**

The journey to the first ₹1 crore is usually the toughest because it relies mostly on **savings, consistency, and patience**, not on compounding. If you invest ₹25,000 per month at 15% annual returns, it takes about **12 years** to reach ₹1 crore. But to reach the **next ₹1 crore**, it takes only around **5 more years,** and the one after that even less.

This shows that **time and compounding** work hardest *after* the first crore — but only if you stay invested long enough to let them.

Reaching the first ₹1 crore helps you instill crucial investing habits:

- **Consistency:** Regular investing through SIPs or disciplined monthly contributions.
- **Delayed gratification:** Learning to prioritize long-term goals over instant rewards.
- **Volatility:** Managing volatility & learning emotional resilience during market downturns.

These habits form the foundation of sustainable wealth creation — habits that serve you far beyond the first milestone.

Once the corpus reaches ₹1 crore, **returns start working harder than new contributions.**

At a 12% annual return, ₹1 crore grows by ₹12 lakh in a year — equivalent to investing ₹1 lakh every month without adding new money. This shift marks a **compounding inflection point,** where wealth starts to multiply faster with less external effort. The investor's role transitions from *building* capital to *protecting and compounding* it.

The first ₹1 crore also delivers **confidence and peace of mind.** It validates years of effort, reinforces faith in the process, and reduces dependence on short-term market movements.

It's often the point where investors stop "chasing returns" and start focusing on **long-term financial independence.** More importantly, it builds emotional stability — the realization that wealth creation is not luck-driven, but behaviour-driven.

Beyond numbers, the first crore is a **launchpad for financial freedom**. It provides options — to take calculated risks, diversify, invest in new asset classes, or even step back from active income if desired. The same habits that helped reach the first crore can now accelerate wealth creation exponentially in the years ahead.

"The first ₹1 crore is the proof of patience; every crore after that is the reward for it."

Key Takeaways

- *Make a beginning with 2-3 good mutual funds, depending upon your risk tolerance – Flexi cap and large cap categories are suitable for most investors*
- *Focus on the size, quality, and track record of the fund, but don't worry too much about the returns in the short term – Good funds deliver benchmark-beating returns in the longer term*
- *I personally prefer multiple funds to avoid intermittent performance issues that most funds experience over time*
- *Focus on creating the first 1 Crore of liquid wealth through regular and consistent investing*
- *Try to adopt step-up investing in line with your income growth, which helps you accumulate a much larger corpus in the longer term – It makes the journey far easier as you increase your investment in line with growth in your income levels so not putting undue pressure on your spending patterns*

Journey of 'Freedom of Choice'

- **First things first**

a. How much is 'Enough' – Finding the 'Magic Number'
b. Understand the basics

- **Executing the Plan**

a. Starting the 'Journey' with a Plan
b. Build a strong foundation
c. Asset Classes & Importance of Equity
d. Where & How to 'Start'
e. Asset Allocation & Timing
f. Importance of Gold in your Journey
g. Golden 'Habits'

- **Avoiding the 'disruptors'**
- **Some practical tips – Experience sharing & Perspective**

EXECUTING THE PLAN: ASSET ALLOCATION & TIMING

Asset allocation involves distributing an investment portfolio across various asset classes, such as stocks, bonds, commodities, real estate, and cash, to balance risk and reward. The goal for asset allocation is to create a diversified portfolio tailored to an investor's unique financial goals, tolerance for risk, and time horizon.

By mixing different assets, which don't always move in the same direction, investors can potentially smooth out market ups and downs and improve long-term returns while minimizing potential losses.

While Asset allocation is important at every stage in life but becomes more critical once you reach a reasonable corpus and as you age. Generally, at the beginning of your investing journey, even an 80-90 % equity allocation is not a bad idea provided you have a longer horizon, and your emergency needs are taken care of through safe debt instruments.

As a thumb rule, don't stress too much about asset allocation in the first 5-7 years of your financial investing journey and increase the emphasis on allocation over time.

It would be critical to manage your allocation based on factors explained before, as you reach a significant corpus (i.e., ~40-50% of your desired corpus for this goal) or you have less than 5-7 years to reach your freedom number, whichever is earlier.

While some guidance recommends that you should hold 100 minus your current age in equities and balance in debt, but this, in my view, is too simplistic and may not work well in each case.

Rather, figuring out your own asset allocation based on the following factors is more appropriate:

- **Risk & Volatility Tolerance**: How much fluctuation (potential notional loss) an investor can emotionally and financially withstand. This is very personal and differs from individual to individual.
  While there is no tool to measure this mental resilience, but I can recommend something simple for most people. Easiest and most practical way to figure out your ability to withstand market volatility is to reflect on your own mindset or emotional reaction to any downturn in the market you might have experienced – If you panicked and started thinking of withdrawing to avoid further drop or did that actually, your resilience is poor but if you saw this as an opportunity and invested more depending upon liquidity, you might have higher tolerance than average investor.

- **Time Horizon & Financial Goals**: The length of time before the investor needs access to the money. Longer time horizons allow for more aggressive (higher-risk) allocations, while shorter horizons call for more conservative (lower-risk) approaches. Therefore, one should move to a higher fixed income allocation (comparatively) as you near your goal of financial freedom. Taking an example of investment done for child education should be moved to fixed income instruments a few years before the need to ensure you don't struggle with market volatility during paying for the intended goal, in case the markets were to go into a bear phase.

Generally speaking, an allocation of 75-80 percent in equity if you have more than 10 years for the intended goal or use of this money is never a bad idea, provided one is prepared for volatility in the interim.

If you find it difficult to assess your situation based on the above, go with the thumb rule of 100 minus your age in equities and balance in Debt and Gold. We will discuss the importance of gold in the next section and how much might be good enough for most people.

Key Takeaways

- *Asset allocation (specifically for a freedom goal) is important but does not matter much at the beginning of your journey*

- *Significant equity allocation (75-80 %) may not be a bad idea, provided you are 10-plus years away from your goal*
- *Over time, adjust your asset allocation based on your risk tolerance or the thumb rule.*
- *Debt and Gold should be part of the asset allocation – In some cases even real estate could be a good option, which should replace debt/ gold rather than equity.*

Journey of 'Freedom of Choice'

❖ **First things first**

a. How much is 'Enough' – Finding the 'Magic Number'
b. Understand the basics

❖ **Executing the Plan**

a. Starting the 'Journey' with a Plan
b. Build a strong foundation
c. Asset Classes & Importance of Equity
d. Where & How to 'Start'
e. Asset Allocation & Timing
f. Importance of Gold in your Journey
g. Golden 'Habits'

❖ **Avoiding the 'disruptors'**

❖ **Some practical tips – Experience sharing & Perspective**

EXECUTING THE PLAN: IMPORTANCE OF GOLD IN YOUR JOURNEY

Gold (or some amount of Silver) is an important part of any long-term portfolio, more for stability than only returns. While this concept of stability vs. returns has been questioned post the unprecedented run that precious metals (gold and silver) experienced over the last couple of years, enhancing the overall long term returns significantly, it remains relevant as a concept considering the historical evidence.

Some of the key reasons gold and silver should be part of your long-term portfolio is explained with a few pointers below:

- **Hedge against Inflation**: Both gold and silver have a long history of retaining their value and purchasing power during inflationary periods when the value of traditional currencies erodes. Gold, in particular, is a strong & consistent performer in this regard.
- **Portfolio Diversification**: The prices of gold and silver generally have a low to negative correlation with stocks, bonds, and other major asset classes. Their inclusion in the portfolio helps reduce overall risk and

volatility, especially during market downturns, and can help offset losses in other asset classes.

- **"Safe Haven"**: During times of geopolitical tension, financial crises, or market turmoil, investors move to gold and silver as reliable, tangible stores of value. This increased demand often causes their prices to rise when other assets are falling, providing a crucial safety net.
- **High Liquidity**: Both gold and silver are globally recognized and highly liquid assets, meaning they can be easily bought or sold for cash when needed. This flexibility provides investors with quick access to funds in emergencies.

I personally prefer a larger gold allocation and a lower silver allocation, primarily due to the much higher volatility in the prices of silver. Silver's dual use as an industrial metal and an investment asset makes its price highly sensitive to economic conditions and market sentiment, leading to sharp price swings that can be much higher than gold.

Generally, 8-10 % of gold or any precious metal could be a reasonable hedge for volatile periods, and anything beyond may not add much value. Having said that, not having gold may not harm any long-term portfolio either, but it is advisable to have some allocation towards these, especially considering the changing world order and conflicts amongst major economic powers. Only exception to this generic rule could be period of high global volatility like wars, conflicts or economic uncertainties in which case, increasing the gold allocation to 15-20% may not be a bad idea provided you understand the cycles well or best would be to rely on an expert.

While Gold & Silver have delivered extraordinary returns over the last couple of years, a good investor is someone who can avoid the recency bias and stay focused on the plan. Overindulgence, based on recency bias, in any asset class, can be harmful to your long-term goals. Let me explain this a bit.

Recency bias in investing is the tendency to give too much weight to recent market performance while making investment decisions, generally ignoring long-term trends and historical data. This behavioural bias can lead to impulsive, emotional choices that harm long-term financial goals by prompting panic selling during downturns or chase "hot" investments during rallies. The second part is what is playing out in Gold and Silver currently, i.e., Q2/Q3 2025

Recency bias can cause investors to abandon a well-defined, long-term investment plan in favour of short-term returns. For example, a mutual fund investor might switch from a diversified fund with a solid track record to a currently popular, but more volatile, fund.

Here is some advice on avoiding recency bias:

Focus on long-term goals: Establish a clear investment strategy tied to your long-term financial goals, such as retirement or financial freedom. Remind yourself of these goals during any temptation to make impulsive, short-term decisions.

Diversify your portfolio: By spreading investments across different asset classes, you can mitigate the risk of overexposure to any single trend. A diversified portfolio is designed to weather market cycles, which helps counteract the impulse to react to the recent performance of just one asset.

Automate investments: Use automatic investment plans, such as a Systematic Investment Plan (SIP) for mutual funds. This enforces discipline by investing regularly, regardless of market conditions, and prevents you from trying to time the market.

Look at long-term data: When evaluating an investment, examine its performance over multiple market cycles (e.g., 1, 3, and 5 years or more) rather than just the last few months. This provides a more balanced view of its consistency and true potential.

Last but not least, a qualified financial advisor can offer an objective assessment of your portfolio and goals. Their perspective is unclouded by emotions and recent market noise, which can help keep your strategy on track. More on choosing the right advisor later.

How to invest in Gold or Silver

When you are buying gold for investment purposes, it's best to avoid physical buying to avoid the risk of theft, storage issues, etc. You could buy gold & silver through multiple modes, though ETFs, Mutual Funds, and Sovereign Gold Bonds (stopped for now) remain my preferred options. Let us understand in brief:

Gold Exchange-Traded Funds (Gold ETFs): These are investment funds that track the price of physical gold. Gold ETFs are traded on stock exchanges just like stocks. One unit of a Gold ETF typically represents a certain quantity of physical gold with high purity held by the fund.

ETFs can be bought and sold using a Demat account during market hours - has no storage or purity concerns compared to physical gold. These are highly liquid and can be liquidated at short notice.

Gold ETF Fund of Funds: These are a type of mutual funds which invest in Gold ETFs. Gold funds pool money from investors to invest in gold through Gold ETFs. You don't need a Demat account for this, and these can be bought like any other mutual fund scheme, including SIP (Systematic Investment Plan) for disciplined investing. Generally, the expense ratio of these funds is higher than that of ETFs.

Taxation for each category differs, and it's important to look at the current regime before taking a call on the type of investment.

Given that Indian households generally hold gold in the form of jewellery as well, which, though not an investment, is rather for personal use, should be considered while calculating your allocation to gold. This is important to avoid over investing into an asset class, which could impact the returns over time.

Key Takeaways

- *Gold (or even silver) could be a good hedge against inflation and helps a diversified portfolio smoothen the returns in the longer term*
- *8-10 % allocation to Gold (including some minor amount to silver as well) is advisable for a well-diversified portfolio*
- *Avoid buying physical gold and prefer exchange-traded funds or gold mutual funds*
- *Gold should be used to replace debt in the portfolio rather than equity*

Journey of 'Freedom of Choice'

❖ **First things first**

a. How much is 'Enough' – Finding the 'Magic Number'
b. Understand the basics

❖ **Executing the Plan**

a. Starting the 'Journey' with a Plan
b. Build a strong foundation
c. Asset Classes & Importance of Equity
d. Where & How to 'Start'
e. Asset Allocation & Timing
f. Importance of Gold in your Journey
g. Golden 'Habits'

❖ **Avoiding the 'disruptors'**

❖ **Some practical tips – Experience sharing & Perspective**

EXECUTING THE PLAN: GOLDEN 'HABITS' BEYOND GOLD

While long term success in wealth creation is dependent on your contributions to the corpus and the time you give it to compound, there are a few habits which help improve the success rate as well as go a long way in fast-tracking this journey.

Staying below your means is the first such habit that will help you stay in control of your finances and catapult your wealth creation journey, in addition to the savings/ investments. Let me elaborate on this before you equate this habit with being a 'miser'. The idea is absolutely not that one shouldn't spend, but luxury has no limits, and staying below your means when you can afford some luxury in life adds up. By all means, follow your passion and spend on what you love, but be conscious of the fact that 'money saved is money earned'. Everyone can implement this in their own way, and there is no magic or 'one size fits all' formula for this.

Some may want to avoid buying a luxury car even when they can afford it, and some could avoid upgrading the phone every second year and rather do it once the phone fails to meet the objectives it is meant for. Small things add up over the long term. A few lakhs saved today would add the same amount every year after a decade of compounding – let this sink in and let me explain.

Year	Amount
0	Amount Invested - 1 Lakh
5	Grows to 2 Lakh
10	Grows to 4 Lakh
15	Grows to 8 Lakh

Assuming 15% CAGR over a longer time horizon.

If you notice, post year 10, you are adding almost 0.8 lakh every year to your wealth, which is almost equal to the initial savings. Now, this will become 1.6 Lakh per year post 15 years of compounding.

So next time, you think of staying below your means, try doing this math and see the perspective change in your mind.

Keep Investing Simple and don't chase every new instrument in the market. There are far too many complex products being sold (or mis-sold) to investors with potentially higher returns, many of which are beyond any common man's circle of competence. In the longer term, it helps to keep investing decisions simple and avoid complexity in any form.

This even applies to equity investing; if you try buying direct stocks, buy businesses that you can understand, and not all the ones that you hear about. Crypto is another example where a lot of money has been made as well as lost, primarily due to a lack of understanding by investors. Not saying, any of these are good or bad but generally keeping investing decisions simple helps avoid risk of capital loss.

Be an optimist when it comes to investing. Optimism makes wealth, and pessimism destroys it. If you are invested in the right assets, remain optimistic about their long-term performance, otherwise, you may exit at the wrong time. People who are optimists believe in the longer-term story and ensure short-term pessimism does not impact their decision-making ability, and they don't end up taking a wrong exit.

Avoid unproductive Debt at any cost. Don't buy depreciating stuff on debt as far as possible. Now this may be slightly controversial as many of us end up buying a car on a loan. Here is the difference: if the car is a need, you are buying within your means, and you can't defer the decision to save enough, go for it, but avoid travel loans, credit card debt at any cost. Buy what you can pay for!

Don't copy your neighbour for any lifestyle needs. Everyone's outlook in life is different, and even the starting points could be different, so it is absolutely fine if you have friends who have a higher lifestyle spending than you. Don't buy stuff based on comparisons; buy based on your needs.

Charlie Munger once said:

'If you live below your means, avoid unnecessary debt, and avoid envy, you will be fine in any era.'

And

Looking rich means debt, envy, and drama, while being rich means freedom, security & peace of mind.'

So, avoid looking rich at any cost and rather focus on being rich.

Key Takeaways

- *Stay below your means, keep investing simple, and don't copy your neighbour*
- *Invest in simple to understand instruments rather than chasing complexity for potentially higher returns*

- *Optimism about future might help you make more wealth in the longer term so don't fear the downcycles in the equity market*

> **Real wealth is what is invisible such as investments and the freedom to leave what you don't like**

Journey of 'Freedom of Choice'

❖ **First things first**

a. How much is 'Enough' – Finding the 'Magic Number'
b. Understand the basics

❖ **Executing the Plan**

a. Starting the 'Journey' with a Plan
b. Build a strong foundation
c. Asset Classes & Importance of Equity
d. Where & How to 'Start'
e. Asset Allocation & Timing
f. Importance of Gold in your Journey
g. Golden 'Habits'

❖ **Avoiding the 'disruptors'**

❖ **Some practical tips – Experience sharing & Perspective**

AVOIDING THE DISRUPTORS:

What could derail your financial Freedom journey

Here are some factors that, in my view, pull you away from your financial Freedom goal.

1. Lifestyle Creep and Moving Targets

The biggest reason for people are unable to reach some form of financial Freedom (partial or full) is not their current earning abilities but rather their constant desire to upgrade based on increased income levels. Now, there is no harm in upgrading your house, car, or any other lifestyle necessity if you have the financial resources to do that and can justify the need to yourself; however, after you hit a baseline in terms of facilities, try prioritising Financial Freedom over any form of upgrade, which only gives you marginal utility beyond a point.

In typical situations, most people end up upgrading their home or car whenever they have the potential to afford something bigger / better without even evaluating the need for it.

This is a killer for the Financial Freedom goal. Now, don't get me wrong, I am not saying that one should not spend/invest towards goals like Housing, Car, Child education, etc. – All I am saying is once you achieve the baseline needs, you should prioritise pushing all your savings towards the Financial Freedom goal before you move the goal post.

Let me give you a practical example of my personal case. I moved into my current house in a decent locality in the city where I worked in 2016. Now, this is a good, well-constructed apartment which meets all my needs of a good community, a good house, and facilities for kids, like a club, sports, swimming pool, etc. Having said that, there is no end to luxury – both in terms of space as well as ambience or facilities, and as our income levels increase, you start to redefine luxury based on what is better available in the market rather than what you really need.

Similarly, as we started living and income levels went up, there were times that we started thinking of upgrading to a bigger house or maybe a more luxurious condominium. This urge, with rising income levels, is very natural, and everyone faces it.

Here are the 2 choices we had:

- Sell the house we stay in, take an additional home loan, or use your savings and get into a new place
- Continue to stay where we are and add on that we can afford in the form of additional EMIs, divert that towards other goals, e.g., Financial Freedom

I chose the second option, which has gone a long way in preponing the achievement of my financial freedom goal – I ended up catching up on my late start through this. I continue to stay in the same house, and my life is pretty good!

The above example can be equally applicable to other lifestyle upgrades like Car etc., but in Indian households (especially higher income professionals in metros), constant housing upgrade is the biggest drain on goals.

Let's take the story forward and assume you also followed the above strategy and achieved your financial freedom, but still have saving potential and an urge to continue working for money. By all means, come back to option 1 above and go ahead and upgrade your lifestyle.

'Whole point is to prioritise Financial Freedom as a goal once you hit the baseline milestones before you move the goal post.'

In most cases, this urge is driven by 2 factors:

- Availability of higher disposable income
- Peer comparison or social pressures

Now, the solution to 1st problem is to divert the savings towards other important goals, which will control that urge. For the second issue, one needs to work on the mindset. It's not always easy, but doable provided you focus on your own game.

As Chuck Palahniuk said:

> *"We buy things we don't need with money we don't have to impress people we don't like."*

How to do is the key question and there is no straight answer however here is something worth attempting - Every time you think of a long term financial commitment on a lifestyle asset, pause for a few weeks and consciously reflect on the number of months/years it can pull you away from your Financial Freedom goal (easiest proxy for this is the number of EMIs if you are going for a leverage) and if you still think it's worth it, Go ahead and execute it but do give time to reflect using some form of yardstick if not the above!

2. Technology upgrades

Technology is changing almost at the speed of light, and our constant desire to keep upgrading faster than you really need is another drain on your resources and can pull you away from your goal. No harm in using a new laptop, Tab or phone, but the frequency of change and marginal utility it provides is worth assessing before you put another lakh on the same every year or in some cases even earlier.

Again, here is something worth trying before the next upgrade - Try identifying 3-5 significant add on features which help you do your job better or make this upgrade a must vs. what you already own (apart from change in the series with higher specs / better looks) - I bet it would be difficult to find the real value applying this test and not upgrading might be a no brainier.

3. Peer comparisons

As they say, no one is unhappy with his / her current state, it's the comparison which makes it difficult - Many of us aspire for a bigger house, better club, faster car or a luxury holiday not just because of our own aspirations but a lot of times due to constant peer comparisons (Includes extended family, friends and even acquaintances) - everyone is running a different race and faster you realise this better it is for your financial goals (and your peace of mind)!

4. Ignorance

How many of us have had a conversation around this in our families - my guess is a few. Talk about financial Freedom as much as you talk about career with your kids/ families. Ignorance of this concept and lack of conscious attempt to include this as a goal in addition to your career goals is one of the biggest contributors to not starting on this journey for many of us - for me, it definitely was at some point, and I wish I knew this in my 20s.

Sounds very basic, yet many of us hardly reflect on this before making long-term financial commitments, and generally, the urge to get a better version of the already owned asset is extremely strong even for a rational mind.

5. Absence of Emergency Fund and Medical Insurance

One of the key pillars of any sound financial plan is the creation of an emergency fund, which helps avoid the urge to dip into the corpus of your financial freedom goal in case of sudden job loss or any other medical or family emergency. Best-made financial plans could get significantly derailed if there are draws midway to support emergency needs. Therefore, to ensure you remain on track to achieve financial freedom as per your plan, always focus on building and maintaining an emergency fund as well as sufficient medical insurance (covering you and your dependent family members).

Quantum of emergency funds depends on your monthly expenses, life stage you are in, and risk of sudden layoffs in your profession, as well as medical needs of your family.

Key Takeaways

- *Know the disruptors, learn more about them, and avoid them to ensure you stay on track for your financial freedom journey*

Lifestyle creep is a silent killer of potential Freedom of Choice

Journey of 'Freedom of Choice'

- **First things first**

a. How much is 'Enough' – Finding the 'Magic Number'
b. Understand the basics

- **Executing the Plan**

a. Starting the 'Journey' with a Plan
b. Build a strong foundation
c. Asset Classes & Importance of Equity
d. Where & How to 'Start'
e. Asset Allocation & Timing
f. Importance of Gold in your Journey
g. Golden 'Habits'

- **Avoiding the 'disruptors'**
- **Some practical tips – Experience sharing & Perspective**

SOME PRACTICAL TIPS – EXPERIENCE SHARING & PERSPECTIVE

Focus on skills & earning potential enhancement in your 20s and 30s

The biggest contributor to any financial goal, let alone financial freedom, is to have a higher savings rate, which is not only a function of optimising spend (Though that has its own advantages) but is rather more directly linked to enhancing your earning ability.

Focus on improving your earnings in the beginning by gaining skills that are in demand and can be monetised. Soft skills, in addition to your technical competence, also add a lot of value to your earning ability or income potential.

The world needs better collaborators, communicators, cross-functional team players, in addition to technical competence. Soft skills open new doors and differentiate you in your current role, impacting your earning ability. There is a general tendency to under-estimate the power of some of these traits. I can tell you with 25 years of my experience working with different teams and corporates, people with better communication and articulation skills grow much faster than the others in most cases – they also get higher responsibilities faster than their cohort because they are more visible with a clear point of view.

Some of the soft skills that one could look at enhancing irrespective of the field you are in, include oral communication, stakeholder management, articulation, collaboration, and structured thinking. Try opting for roles that help you grow in these areas in addition to your field of expertise.

Stock Options (ESOPs) vs. Bigger pay cheque

Many of us are sometimes faced with a choice between a role/job with a higher cash salary vs. something that offers lower cash but includes ESOPs. While one cannot generalise this advice, if you are convinced of the business model and ability of the enterprise as well as its founding team to excel and have a longer runway in terms of your career (more applicable for starters – I would definitely ask my son to evaluate this with a different lens than I did), it would generally be better to bet on ESOPs than just cash. The advantage with such roles is that the wealth creation can be much larger if the entity grows, and, in a way, you can influence that growth with your hard work. As I said, while it may not be fair to generalise this, but in my practical experience, ESOPs fast-track your journey to financial freedom not only because rise in value but because of certain softer aspects which work favourably with human behaviour, i.e.

- ESOPs of early-stage entities generally don't have liquidity, hence you by default end up holding them longer, which addresses the biggest behavioural issue of not giving time to an asset to grow.
- The growth rates in early-stage entities are far higher than the regular 12-15% growth of established entities, and hence if all goes well and you stick around, your CAGR potentially could be double that, which can reduce the time you need to achieve your goals. Now, you understand the basics and can easily extrapolate the impact of higher returns in the longer term.
- You can influence the growth of the entity as one of the participants, i.e., you control your destiny (to a limited extent, maybe, but that helps), and if you work well and hard, it fast-tracks your financial freedom journey.

This does not mean that every ESOP opportunity is worth jumping at – Do consider the quality of the founder, business model, quality of investors, and your alignment with the business goals before you take any such opportunity. Sometimes, a bird in hand is better than two in the bush, so evaluate carefully but prioritise ESOPs if all other things seem exciting.

Don't stress too much about the Future & Keep working on your present

Let me explain this with a story (and a real one) which might convey this better than a paragraph in plain English.

On one of the weekends, we were driving towards Delhi. While we crossed Medanta (a large hospital in Gurgaon, the city I live in), I suddenly felt some breathlessness and for a minute felt that I was having a heart attack – Seems stupid now, but I did panic. As I experienced this, my mind started creating all kinds of scenarios about the future. So, I immediately told my wife to drive and take me straight to the emergency, and the next moment I was in the triage of the emergency, where ECG / some tests were conducted. Now, while I was waiting for the results, an old gentleman approached me who was accompanying his wife to the emergency.

By his own admission, he was around 75-year-old and was a retired physician. He might have been curious to see someone young and not so sick (on the face of it, at least) lying in an emergency bed, building scenarios with a blank face. I must admit, he was one of the happiest and most jovial people I have ever met. While I explained my story, he said I have been a doctor with experience in treating patients for 40+ years and can tell you, seeing your face, there is nothing wrong with your heart – you panicked and the future planning increased your anxiety.

It relieved me, but I remained tense till the results came in. The results confirmed his diagnosis an hour later. Realising that I was very tense in the moment, this is the wisdom he shared, which left a profound impact on me:

"Son - In my 75+ years of life, I have never thought about the next moment and haven't looked back even a second – and it's been a wonderful journey". Easy – Not really. Possible – Absolutely!

I haven't been able to fully inculcate this habit in me (though I do wish to make this a reality & have been working towards it through mindfulness practice). Here is some advice for me & you:

- *Train your mind to observe more and stay in the present moment. As per a study, an average human's mind is wandering ~ 47 percent of the time in a day. It would be much higher for me & you in this digitally connected world –* ***Remain mindful of now!***
- *Developing some form of faith in the higher power managing this universe helps to avoid analysis of the past and scenario building of the future ('What if' analysis for the consulting folks) – Try this, it works! -* **Don't Regret the past & Worry about the future.**

This is easier said than done, given that the human mind is a Monkey but try trying and don't keep thinking about the large financial freedom number all the time😊.

Small Habits compound

Another extremely practical but often missed opportunity is the impact of small habit changes, which compound over time. Let me give you some relatable examples specially for people in metros. Eating out is a significant spend in most cases (try capturing the spend in your spend tracker if you haven't, and you might be surprised with the number – It's almost equal to your regular kitchen/ grocery spend), and it's unavoidable given the lifestyle we have, routine stress levels and need of some break from routine/monotony.

Having said that, visiting a fine dining place regularly could be draining for your finances. Just by avoiding (or reducing the number of visits) fine dining places (typically 50% more expensive), you could still fulfil your family's urge for eating out but reduce your monthly spend.

Another tiny habit which helps in the long term is tracking your expenses – It is much easier now with so many mobile-based tracking Apps. I have done this for a long time (though I must admit, I have only done this inconsistently) and have been surprised by some of the findings which helped me make changes to my lifestyle. Another extremely important element is that when you start tracking, you become mindful of the spending, and it automatically helps to avoid some of the wasteful expenditure.

Find an 'Advisor without conflict.'

Let me explain this. I have already explained the need for an advisor at multiple places already and don't think I can emphasize more on the importance of a good advisor/mentor. But the challenge is that when you look at advisors in the market, most of us misunderstand or confuse mutual fund distributors and insurance sellers as advisors, which they are not. They always have a conflict of interest when they are recommending something to you, and the advice is not necessarily sound financial advice for your end goals.

Here is what helps if you are not financially savvy: Look for a good Registered Investment Advisor (fewer than 1000 registered ones are available as per some data) and get a plan created based on your goals. They will charge you for a plan but might give you sound advice free of conflicts.

While searching for an advisor/partner, don't get carried away by people who claim to offer the highest returns in the short run or those who claim to be smart enough at predicting market cycles (no one can, and anyone who claims this is best avoided for a better financial journey). Rather, search for an advisor who can work with you during the chaos (COVID was a period of chaos) and keeps you focused on long term compounding rather than asking you to chase every new trend in the market.

Do-it-yourself (DIY) investing is not suitable for most investor due to various reasons like:

- **Fear, greed, and herd mentality** can lead to impulsive decisions like panic-selling in a market crash or chasing hot stocks. Without discipline, emotions often override logic, hurting long-term returns.
- **Long-Term Discipline:** Staying invested for 15–20 years requires patience and discipline. Many DIY investors drop out midway due to a lack of conviction in their strategy.
- **A DIY investor may not have the same depth of understanding,** which can lead to poor stock selection, over-diversification, or concentration risk.
- **Poor Risk Management:** DIY investors often fail to protect downside, especially during market corrections.
- **Analysis Paralysis:** With too much information (YouTube, Twitter, blogs, stock tips), DIY investors may freeze, delaying decisions or making inconsistent ones.

The above are softer aspects, and there are other more compelling reasons like tax efficiency of decisions, liquidity, etc., which a good advisor can help with.

Do 'Nothing'

While this is true for all sound investments but specifically helpful in case you are largely invested in the equity markets. Stock markets go through cycles and are influenced by multiple global and local factors apart from the core business. These cycles work in both directions, markets will run faster than you imagined, potentially pushing your mind to encash the investments, and on the other hand, sometimes the markets will fall significantly (COVID, US imposed Tariffs being some of the recent examples), prompting you to cash out and avoid further drop (mostly temporary volatility) in capital.

In such situations, generally 'doing nothing' works the best in the long run as you cannot time any of the cycles. **If you have time at hand (more than 5 years), generally, just sitting tight, ignoring all the noise, and doing nothing is the best strategy for long term success.**

I have seen enough examples where people encashed their long-term savings due to market rise or fall, with an idea to get in once markets cool off or stabilise, but missed out on long-term compounding.

Charlie Munger puts this very aptly

> *"Never interrupt the compounding unnecessarily."*

Act like 'Dead' & Forget about investments

One of Fidelity's most famous and widely cited finding suggests that the best-performing client accounts belonged to people who had either forgotten they had an account or were deceased. This illustrates the powerful effect of not reacting to short-term market changes.

Behavioural psychology reflects the concept of "myopic loss aversion," which is the human tendency to overreact to market losses, even when an investment's long-term outlook is positive. Reacting emotionally to downturns often causes investors to sell at low points, locking in losses.

Staying invested during downturns

A 2015 Fidelity study of 1.5 million workplace retirement savers demonstrated the long-term rewards of staying in the market during the 2008–2009 financial crisis. In the decade following the crisis, those who stayed invested saw their account balances grow by 147%. This was double the 74% return for those who fled stocks during the downturn. Over 25% of the investors who sold their stocks never re-entered the market and missed out on the subsequent gains.

Disciplined, long-term investing & Asset Allocation

Fidelity's research also supports the idea that discipline and a long-term plan are more important than attempting to "time" the market.

According to Fidelity, strategic asset allocation—the mix of stocks, bonds, and cash—is the single most important factor influencing a portfolio's long-term risk and return.

Research cited by Fidelity suggests that asset allocation is responsible for more than 90% of the variability in a portfolio's returns.

Buy the 'Bad News'

If you are invested in the equity markets and have a horizon longer than 10 years, buy your favourite funds at every bad news. Markets give you opportunities over time, and people who fear these opportunities get the usual market returns, while people who embrace these as opportunities to invest more end up making better than normal returns over time. Classic and recent examples of this are the COVID period. Anyone who liquidated their investment fearing fall (specifically the corpus meant for long-term goals) permanently lost anywhere between 20-40% capital, while people who used this as an opportunity to step up investment have made more than 25% XIRR over the next 4-5 years. This is more recent, but data will tell you that this is generally the case.

The only thing one should be cautious of is the time available. If your goals are nearing, avoid this, but given that we are discussing financial freedom and long-term investing, this rule holds in almost all situations. So, go long on every abnormal fall due to 'Bad News'. My returns on fresh funds deployed during COVID look higher than the average despite the markets giving almost NIL returns in last more than a year.

Warren Buffett has captured this aptly:

> *'Be fearful when others are greedy, and be greedy when others are fearful.'*

Avoid losing capital

It seems extremely simple, and one would argue why this is even worth discussing – Isn't it too basic to understand that one should never lose money? Let me explain the reason why this is critical for anyone, specifically an equity investor, from a behavioural point of view, rather than just the capital loss which you can still recover from with better earning/savings.

Losing capital in the market pushes you away from equities as an asset class, and you sometimes become ultra conservative, impacting your long-term compounding story. I know someone who invested heavily in the equity markets and had built a reasonable portfolio, but then someone advised him to try F&O (Futures and Options) to make quicker gains. He tried and not only did he fail miserably, but he lost significant capital. This led to complete confidence loss for him, and he became ultra conservative and only invests in Bank Deposits now. He has retired at the age of 50 with zero exposure to equity – while things are fine for now, but I fear his capital will not be able to keep pace with inflation and he will suffer in the long run.

Such behavioural shift is avoidable if you don't overexpose yourself and don't do things that you don't understand or things that have a risk of capital loss (not volatility but permanent capital loss).

Try 'Minimalism' if you like

This is what I realised during COVID, which left a huge impression on my thinking:

Joy of living with less is unparalleled ('LESS IS MORE)

- 'NIL' discretionary shopping and eating out, which surprisingly (really !) had 'Zero' impact on any of our abilities – I always felt we can't survive without this
- Far more focus on work & personal time as there is less energy on paying for unnecessary bills, figuring out returns, trying to fit extras in already full cupboards, overeating, etc
- Just getting the basics, which is proving to be more than enough for a happy life – Quick calculation suggests more than 50% (if not more) of routine spending is absolutely avoidable

Here is something I tried, which helped control my spending (with some marginal success, though):

Project 333 (Originated by Ms. Courtney Carver, author of a wonderful book called 'Soulful Simplicity' – Worth a read if you like minimalism as a concept) i.e. Try living with 33 clothing items (including shoes, accessories etc.) for 3 months – Seems simple, just try giving it a shot and you will be amazed. To begin with, just count the total items you use currently – I am embarrassed to tell mine!

Key Takeaways

- *Don't stress too much about the future and keep doing what feels right in the present*
- *Avoid losing capital during investing decisions – You may not be able to visualise its impact on your self confidence as well as it might negatively impact your views on a good asset class due to some short term bad decisions*

'Do Nothing' and 'Act like Dead' in Equity Investing

The 'End Game'

a. *Courage to do 'more' of what you 'desire' & 'less' of what just made 'money'*

b. *What not to do once you hit your 'Freedom number'*

c. *Strategy for Withdrawals*

COURAGE TO DO 'MORE' OF WHAT YOU 'DESIRE' & 'LESS' OF WHAT JUST MADE 'MONEY'

There are 2 big steps to really achieve financial freedom, and using the time to your advantage in reality, i.e.

Step 1: Achieving the magic number

Step 2: Courage to exit the race to do 'more' of what you 'desire' & 'less' of what you did for 'money'

While most people fail at step 1, which is about achieving the magic number due to multiple reasons, starting with lack of planning to continuous lifestyle creep, an equal number of people don't muster the courage to take step 2, despite having achieved the required corpus and continue to do what 'pays the best'. They are never able to muster the courage to 'jump the treadmill' due to social pressures and 'some more' mindset, i.e., typical accumulation mindset.

What I have realised over time is that Enough is actually not only a number but rather a feeling which can only come provided you are content with what you have and don't keep moving the goal post.

There is no harm in building a margin for safety beyond the financial freedom number, but never-ending accumulation does not help anyone. Having said that, it is not easy to leave a well-paying job or profession and try something new, and it needs a lot of conviction in the first place. Achieving financial freedom (step 1 above) is half the battle, and balance depends on how well you prepare yourself to 'let go'. While I also don't deny the fact that fear and anxiety are absolutely usual in such a scenario.

Now, let me come back to the starting point of this book, where we discussed 3 key points, and try sharing my real-life example to see if that helps you get a perspective on the end game. As I said, while it's critical to get to the magic number, all this effort would go to waste if you don't use this to 'own your time'.

The idea is just to provide a perspective and broaden your thinking rather than give you a prescription, which is impossible given the diversity of human nature – What excites me may not excite you. In fact, the whole point is that we need to stop believing that there is only one way of living life, i.e., work till 60 and then retire to take care of your grand kids!

There could be mini-retirements or even start-up ideas you may want to explore on the way, and you never know what could turn out to be your Ikigai!

Let's answer the 3 questions with some practical life lessons:

1. Enough Financial Resources to take that risk

As I said, I realised this much later in life that Financial freedom has to be one of the key goals, and hence my journey has some very important lessons to learn from.

Lesson 1: The earlier you start, the easier it will be. The biggest trick in my view is to just assume that you may not want to work in a 9-5 role forever and hence need to sustain with your savings. Now, you may or may not need this corpus for the same purpose and may end up doing working in a 9-5 role till 60 – but, hey, does the extra money harm anyone? You may actually do a world trip if not something else!

So just start with that assumption, and I can tell you with almost certainty that most of us would end up hating the routine after a point and may want to try (if not do) something else.

Lesson 2: Keep your game unique and don't try matching every other guy you meet on the street.

Frame your needs and desires based on what gives you joy and not what makes your neighbour envious.

This is easier said than done, but it is doable provided you control your emotions!

Once in a while you would slip (we are all humans end of the day) and its fine till the time it's an iPhone upgrade and not a Farmhouse that you end up buying based on peer pressures (with EMIs lasting for 25-year 😊) – So in nutshell even if you slip, let that not be life threatening (read 'Freedom Threatening') episode. Don't get too bothered by smaller mistakes and keep the end goal intact!

In my own case, I haven't done a single upgrade based on comparisons but have done many upgrades otherwise, which is just being human. Anytime, I get carried away, I remind myself what I would value more in a few years – 'Freedom of choice' or the 'upgrade', and the answer is generally a writing on the wall!

Let me share a brief story that I wrote about one of the long-distance runs:

Some years ago, I participated in a 10.5 km run, and as part of it, we had to run 5.25 kms in one direction and then take a U-turn to return. As I was reaching the U-turn, I found many runners already returning, so they were much faster than me / ahead of me. In real life too, this happens with us many a times, but it's always better to focus on your own race and keep in mind that everyone has a unique game – if you focus on your game and stop comparing, you would in the end be happy with your own performance!

Lesson 3: It is never enough unless you decide it's enough. The human mind is an expert on moving goal posts and creating fear in every situation. If you ask multiple people who achieved Financial Freedom, you will hear them say that they changed their calculation of the magic number at least 2-3 times before they felt it was enough.

Enough is not a number in reality, it's actually more of a mindset that needs to overcome the fear of the future.

Now, I am not saying, do this casually, but don't overthink and delay what you love doing once you reach the stage after years of planning.

2. *Prioritise your chosen path - Don't stress too much about the social opinion*

We all live in a society that thrives on comparisons and show off – The tendency is generally to keep comparing with people doing better than you financially. This will happen when you decide to leave the race, which is very natural.

The best trick to avoid this is to look at people not as 'well to do' as you are, rather than always looking upwards. Some might argue that this would be counterintuitive to growth because you end up stretching yourself looking at achievers who have done better than you. Now, here is the thing - you do this till you reach the Freedom number by all means, but avoid this as you come closer to the freedom goal.

Otherwise, you would never be able to let go of the peer pressures and social comparisons. I stopped comparing with people who were doing better than me once I reached my financial freedom goal! It is more of a mindset game, and the easiest way is to look downwards than upwards – Look at the comforts and conveniences you have got vs. many others, and you would start to realise how kind God has been to you and your family, and take the plunge, if you like!

3. *Find something meaningful and satisfying if money wasn't the only criterion to choose*

Most of us have hidden desires that get suppressed due to the pressures of earning a livelihood, and if you dig deeper, you would find a few things for sure that you may want to do if the need for money is sorted - if you can't, then keep searching till you get the answer.

In my own case, I had a desire to spend more time in the Mountains and one of the key reasons for me to fast-track my journey of financial independence was to be able to spend more time in our small hill home, which we as a family built with a lot of passion. So I started to find ways that would keep me engaged in a remote hill town!

Not everyone will have the same desire to slow down; some may want to build a multi-million-dollar enterprise. Even that would require them to execute their start-up idea, which cannot be done unless they have taken care of their bills in the absence of a regular income flow.

One of the easiest ways to catapult your financial freedom journey is to find your passion and make that the centre point of all your decisions – I can guarantee, once you do that, you will end up achieving financial freedom much faster than you can imagine.

TIP:

- *Most people try searching for something meaningful which could replace their level of income which makes the decision to try something new almost impossible. Once you achieve the freedom number, focus on finding your 'Ikigai' and just look at replacing your cost of living to begin with and not the whole income. If you do this, it becomes easier to handle and your freedom corpus compounds and becomes your backup plan.*

Key Takeaways

- *As you work on your financial freedom number, develop courage to 'let go' and work on your ability to chose a path of your desires without worrying about societal pressures – I can tell you with confidence, Mindset change is the hardest of the two*

Enough is less of a number & more of a mindset. Build courage to do 'more' of your 'desire' & 'less' of what you did for 'money'

The 'End Game'

a. *Courage to do 'more' of what you 'desire' & 'less' of what just made 'money'*
b. *What not to do once you hit your 'Freedom number'*
c. *Strategy for Withdrawals*

WHAT NOT TO DO ONCE YOU HIT YOUR 'FREEDOM NUMBER'

Avoid catastrophic risks with your capital: Once you hit your freedom number, avoid risking your capital at any cost. Preserve what you have and let the compounding work. The tendency to make more money when you have time and capital is overpowering even for a rational mind. I have seen many people losing capital through Derivatives and Trading – It all starts with the urge to make more money, but ends up badly for most people.

As per SEBI data, 9 out of 10 traders in the equity futures and options segment in Indian markets lost money. Now, that's a staggering number, with 90 percent of people losing money. This, in my view, is closest to gambling than to investment. Don't get carried away by such money-making (or rather losing) strategies.

This is more critical for people who achieve financial freedom with a lot of discipline in their 40s, as the runway left to cover up for any misadventure is lesser. Any mistake in your 20s has a much longer corrective window, but not when you are in your 40s or 50s. Any decision with a risk of permanent capital loss should be a 'No-go'.

Manage Tax outflows: Look for better withdrawal strategies and optimise tax outgo on your profits. Systematic Withdrawal Plan or even dividend option, if your income is less than the threshold, works well.

Avoid Overexposure to Equities

While this is very individual-driven and there is no perfect answer to the amount of equity you should hold post financial freedom, it depends on multiple factors, let us take a couple of scenarios and try understanding this.

Generally, the studies on retirement planning have recommended a mix of 50/50 debt/equity once you start to use your corpus for withdrawals, but given that we are not talking about retirement, rather freedom to choose, you could look at a higher equity exposure in the following scenarios:

- You will continue to earn from some passion projects or from freelancing even if you stop working full-time once you achieve Financial Freedom. In this scenario, given that you are not looking at withdrawal from your corpus to support your lifestyle completely, you may want to retain a higher equity exposure to get the advantage of long-term compounding.

- You are early to achieve financial freedom (around 45 years or less) and have a lot of time ahead of you still.

Financially secure people tend to be more courageous while making career decisions. Therefore, go ahead and take that career shift or change you always wanted, and don't avoid it any further.

Key Takeaways

- *Avoid any catastrophic risk with your capital post achieving financial freedom*
- *Manage your equity exposure as per your risk taking ability and avoid over-exposure*

The 'End Game'

a. *Courage to do 'more' of what you 'desire' & 'less' of what just made 'money'*
b. *What not to do once you hit your 'Freedom number'*
c. *Strategy for Withdrawals*

STRATEGY FOR WITHDRAWALS

While there are multiple ways one could utilise the corpus, e.g. Buying a fixed rate annuity, investing in cash-generating assets, two most talked about and tested withdrawal strategies are the **Systematic Withdrawal Plan** (SWP) and **Bucket Strategy.** Both of them have their own pros and cons, and depending upon your individual needs, you could look at using either of them.

Let me try explaining both before we conclude which one is more suitable for what kind of situations.

Bucket Strategy involves dividing your freedom corpus into 3-4 distinct buckets— Emergency Needs, Liquid, Income, and Growth—based on different time horizons. This helps manage liquidity for immediate expenses, generate a steady income stream for the medium term, and ensure your savings keep pace with inflation over the long run.

The strategy offers a more effective approach than simply parking the entire corpus in low-return, fixed-income options, which can fail to beat rising inflation.

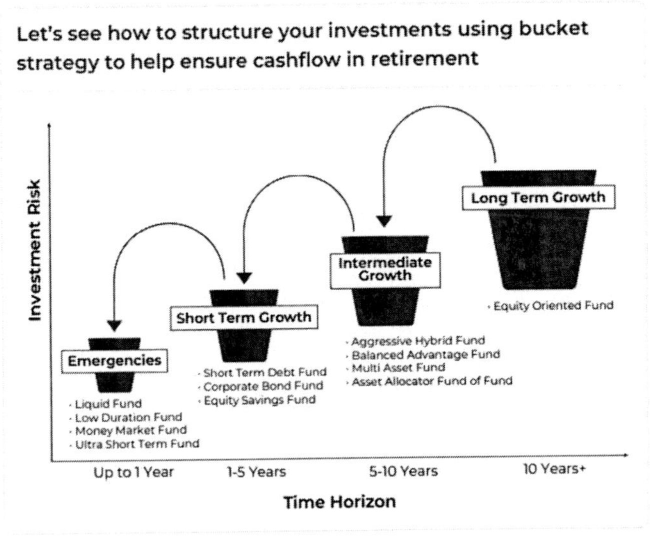

Source: HDFC Mutual Fund

Bucket 1: Emergencies (0-1 Year)

This is your safety net. You can park funds here for emergencies like hospital bills, unexpected expenses, etc. This bucket should be liquid, accessible, and less risky. Some of the Investment options include: Liquid Fund, Low Duration Fund, Money Market Fund, and Ultra Short-Term Fund.

Bucket 2: Short-Term Growth (1-5 Years)

This bucket helps in taking care of your near-term goals or predictable expenses like travel, home repairs, gifting, or topping up your income. Some of the Investment options include: Short Term Debt Fund, Corporate Bond Fund, Equity Savings Fund. Think of it as your income bucket

Bucket 3: Intermediate Growth (5-10 Years)

This bucket is for medium-term growth. It takes a blended approach – a mix of equity and debt. It's meant to grow steadily, so you can refill your first two buckets when needed. Some of the Investment options include: Aggressive Hybrid Fund, Balanced Advantage Fund, Multi-Asset Fund, and Asset Allocator Fund of Funds. Let this bucket breathe – Consider withdrawing from this bucket only in case of emergencies

Bucket 4: Long-Term Growth (10+ Years)

This is your future-focused bucket – meant for legacy planning or for expenses far down the road. It involves equity investments that aim to grow your wealth over time. Some of the Investment options include: Flexi Cap Fund, Large Cap Fund, and Multi Cap Fund.

If the market falls, don't worry - This bucket has time on its side.

Some of the advantages of this strategy are:

- *No panic selling* – Your Immediate needs are covered, so you don't withdraw long-term investments during market volatility

- *Flexibility* – Adjust allocations as your goals change (e.g., shift more to bucket 2 & 3 as you age)
- *Growth + Stability* – Short-term buckets help in providing stability, while long-term buckets could grow your wealth over time.
- As your life changes, your buckets can be adjusted. You might move funds from one bucket to another as you get older or your goals shift. The key is balance and flexibility – You're in control with the freedom to ensure your money works for you, not the other way around.

SWP or Systematic Withdrawal Plan is an approach of withdrawing money periodically from an existing investment, typically a Hybrid or Equity mutual fund. This facility (SWP) is offered by mutual funds that allow investors to withdraw a fixed amount of money at regular intervals (monthly, quarterly, or annually) from their investment. It is the reverse of a Systematic Investment Plan (SIP) – instead of investing periodically, you redeem units systematically.

Some of the advantages of an SWP approach are:

Tax Efficiency: Only capital gains on redeemed units are taxed, not the full withdrawal amount. Further, Long-term capital gains (after 1 year in equity funds) enjoy favourable tax rates specifically for hybrid and equity-only mutual funds.

Flexibility: You can start, stop, or modify SWP anytime — no penalties or lock-ins generally for most schemes, provided the corpus is more than a year old at least.

Continued Compounding: The unwithdrawn corpus remains invested, allowing compounding to continue, which helps grow the remaining capital.

Some of the disadvantages of an SWP approach are:

Risk of Capital Erosion: If withdrawals exceed the fund's returns, your principal may reduce over time, which should not be an issue in the longer term but might make some people uncomfortable seeing their corpus deplete.

Market Volatility: In equity-oriented funds, poor market phases can deplete the corpus faster, which is also called the sequence of returns risk.

Let's draw a simple table comparing the two for a sharper understanding:

Feature	Systematic Withdrawal Plan (SWP)	Bucket Strategy
Portfolio Structure	A single but diversified portfolio	Multiple segregated "buckets" based on the time horizon of need

Withdrawal Mechanism	Fixed withdrawals from the whole portfolio on a defined periodicity	Withdrawals are made from the most liquid short-term bucket first
Market Volatility	Higher psychological stress as the total value fluctuates	Lower stress for immediate needs from liquid funds
Management	Simpler to set up and maintain.	Requires periodic review and manual intervention

Key Takeaways

- *As I said in the beginning, the best choice depends on individual risk tolerance, involvement in the market, and behaviour. For those who panic during market swings or volatility and prefer seeing their corpus more stable in the short term, the bucket strategy offers significant psychological benefits.*
  Grab your buckets, fill them wisely, and enjoy the freedom that comes with knowing your financial future could be solidly prepared, secured, and ready for whatever comes next!
- *On the other hand, SWP might be suitable for those who prefer a simpler, hands-off approach – Key point is one should be fine with the volatility as the corpus could swing in the short term, leading to panic amongst some investors.*

Seek expert advice: For a personalized plan, consult a SEBI-registered financial advisor. Treat this as the summary of the section 😊

REFERENCES USED & USEFUL TOOLS

Some Useful references used in the Book

- Determining Withdrawal Rates using Historical Data by Mr. William Bengen (Famously known as the 4% Rule)
- "Retirement Spending: Choosing a Sustainable Withdrawal Rate," by Philip L. Cooley, Carl M. Hubbard, and Daniel T. Walz (Professors at Trinity University in Texas)
- Balancing Acts: Safe Withdrawal Rates in the Indian Context (Rajan Raju and Ravi Saraogi, CFA) – Jan 2004
- The State of Retirement Income: 2024 (Morningstar)
- Investor Survey 2025 (SEBI)

Tools & Calculators

Below are some of the options that I found useful – These are not my recommendations, but rather the ones I have used and found good. There are many good ones on the net which are free to use, and it's best to explore a few and use the one that works for your situation.

Some of the calculators (especially dealing with financial freedom or FIRE) would give you varied results based on their own logic. It's recommended to follow some of the established advice based on published research or follow a qualified advisor rather than rely on just the calculator.

- **Expense Tracking App**
  - Spending Tracker – Budget App (LightByte Co.)
- **SIP, Step up SIP and SWP Calculators**
  - https://zerodha.com/calculators
- **Freedom Number Calculator**
  - https://www.motilaloswal.com/calculators/fire-calculator
  - Retirement Calculator – Plan Your Retirement Smartly | NISM

CONCLUSION & SUMMARY

Financial freedom is not only a destination — it is a journey of discipline, awareness, and choice. It begins the day you decide to take control of your money instead of letting money control you. Therefore, the first and foremost part of this journey is a shift in mindset and making a beginning.

- **Mindset shift is critical**
  True wealth starts in the mind. Changing how you think about money — from fear to confidence, from consumption to creation — is the foundation of every financial success story. Without the right mindset, even high income leads to dependency. On the other hand, even a modest income can create independence. Discuss Financial Freedom and the path to it more often in your family and with your children. Make this a dinner table conversation rather than a taboo.
- **Start Early, Save Consistently**
  Time is your biggest ally when it comes to investing and growing wealth for financial freedom. The earlier you start saving and investing, the lighter your financial journey becomes. Don't wait for a "big day" or higher income — the habit of saving consistently, even if small, matters more than the amount. Consistency

compounds faster than perfection. Don't chase returns, just follow a consistent process and give money time.

Your journey to financial independence begins with one powerful choice: to start NOW.

- **Your preferences evolve as you grow**
  It is almost impossible for most of us to figure out our Ikigai in the beginning, and as life evolves, our preferences also continue to change. Don't be under the impression that your current lifestyle and work routine will continue to excite as you grow. A change of heart at some stage of life is not unusual, and people who prepare for exploring life end up being happier as they can choose to do what they desire.

Do not think of freedom as retirement, rather think of it as your reason to *gain control of your time* and not be dependent on a paycheque for survival

- **Financial Freedom does not mean retirement**

You may continue to be fully or partially engaged post achieving financial freedom, sometimes in the same profession if you enjoy what you do. Financial Freedom just activates choices in life, and you don't have to pick the work that pays the best, you could own your time. You might even want to have a mini-break to explore a few things in life.

- **Financial Freedom is a must** (even if you don't wish to retire)
  Make financial freedom a career goal much earlier than your retirement plan and try to use this stage to gain control over your schedule. This stage allows you to experiment and explore opportunities without worrying about money. That is its biggest dividend.
- **Invest with a Purpose**
  Wealth grows when money works for you. Build productive assets — equities, businesses, real estate — that generate income even when you don't. Avoid speculation; embrace long-term investing. Trading may give you short-term success, but the momentum does not last. Investing is the only way to make money grow.
- **Money will never be enough unless you consciously decide**
  There are many calculators that one can use on the internet explaining how much is enough for you to sustain a decent lifestyle without worrying about wealth, but let me tell you, enough is not only a mathematical number, but rather it is an emotion to live life on your own terms. If you continue to chase more, it will never be enough. If you enjoy that chase enough, keep going, but if you don't, you should try building a choice of purpose-driven living.

Building a strong foundation goes a long way in ensuring your long-term goals stay on track and don't get impacted by short-term bumps & emergencies of life.

- **Be Financially Literate** (Understand Basics of Money & Investing)
  It is equally important for everyone to be financially literate, irrespective of their educational background or field of work. It is important to understand money and investing to make this part of your core life skills. Financially literate individuals make better investors and end up growing their wealth over time. Even if you use an advisor, make sure you don't fear finance & investing, but rather try getting involved in the process. Being financially literate does not mean you have to be an expert at investing; rather, this means you can understand the investing options and can understand the choices being made (even if by an expert), as well as the journey better.
  This is one of the life skills almost comparable to cooking to survive and goes a long way in making your overall journey smoother and independent.
- **Build a strong foundation - Protect and Plan**
  A sound financial plan includes safety nets — insurance, emergency funds, and debt management. Freedom is not just about wealth; it's about peace of mind and resilience against life's uncertainties.

Developing some Golden 'Habits' & knowing the 'Disruptors' helps you stay on track. Focus on them in addition to improving your earning and savings rate as you go through this journey of financial freedom.

- **Live Below, Grow Beyond**
  Avoid lifestyle inflation and comparison-driven spending. Financial freedom is about options, not opinions. Spend consciously, invest regularly, and let compounding do the quiet work.
  "Financial freedom isn't about having more money — it's about having more control, more time, and more peace."
  Start small. Stay consistent. Think long-term.

- **Try to be an Optimist, Always**
  Optimism makes wealth, and pessimism destroys it. If you are invested in the right assets, remain optimistic about their long-term performance; otherwise you may exit at the wrong time. People who are optimists believe in the longer-term story and ensure short-term pessimism does not impact their decision-making ability, and they don't end up taking a wrong exit.
- **Play your own game and avoid Comparisons**
  Do not aspire for a bigger house, better club, faster car, or a luxury holiday just because of constant comparisons – Keep your race and life purpose unique – the more you imbibe this better your financial journey will turn

out to be. Don't copy your neighbour and be happy with your unique desires.

- **Don't stress about the future**
  The future is brighter than you think, and living in the present is the only way one can stay happy and enjoy a meaningful life. Train your mind to observe more and stay in the present moment

Go beyond just the magic number – Half the journey is reaching the goal, and half is to build courage to do what you desire.

- **Focus on your 'Desires' more than 'Money'**
  Achieving the magic number of about 25-30 times of your annual spend is important for freedom but in addition, you must muster enough courage to follow your heart. It could be working on your passions, your start-up idea, or just spending time with your loved ones, once you reach the magic number. While many would fail to build the required corpus for freedom, an equal number would also not be able to take the final step of exploring their 'Ikigai' and continue to accumulate more even after hitting the required corpus. Enough is not a mathematical number but rather an emotional state when you are ready to work on your desires without worrying about money.
- **Avoid catastrophic risks with Capital**
  Avoid taking risks with your capital once you reach your freedom goal. Losing money needs to be avoided

at any cost. This is more critical for people who achieve financial freedom with a lot of discipline in their 40s, as the runway left to cover up for any misadventure is lesser.

ACKNOWLEDGEMENTS

The idea of this book has been brewing in my mind for a very long time. While I kept delaying this, given my work routine but always felt that once I initiate, this would be quite easy given the learnings I have had over time. Contrary to my long-time belief, writing this book has been a journey of self-reflection and enormous learning for me personally.

This book would not have been possible without the support, wisdom, and encouragement of many people who shaped both the ideas within these pages and me as an individual.

First and foremost, I am deeply grateful to my wife, Neha, whose understanding, constant encouragement, and unwavering belief gave me the strength to keep writing even on the longest and sometimes not very encouraging days. She has been the ghost proof-reader of multiple drafts of this final creation and helped me correct my mistakes (usual for her to find mistakes in me) – She insisted that I write this unambiguously 😊

It's a joke, so don't take this too seriously.

Both my kids, Nehit and Aarshia, took a very keen interest in the contents as well as the flow of this book from the initiation of this idea. Despite their limited financial exposure given the age, they shared some outstanding ideas which helped me enhance the structure as well as the contents of this book. Their love and curiosity kept me going as I was writing my manuscript, which went through many ups and downs.

As a first-time author, I have relied heavily on the feedback and constructive criticism of some of my dear friends whose intellect and life learnings not only enhanced the usefulness of this book but will also ensure this final version adds value to the reader.

For this, I am specifically grateful to my childhood friend & companion, Manoj Marwah, and my dear friend Amit Chand. Both of them have a unique ability to objectively assess every situation in life, a skill I have always admired. I cannot thank them enough for their help in fine-tuning this book before it could reach the editorial team. It has been my privilege that they agreed to spend their valuable time on the draft of this book (despite their busy careers) as this was taking shape. Another very dear childhood mate, Nitin Hans, also deserves a special mention as he helped validate the idea and shared insights on the coverage to enhance its usefulness for the target audience - I remain grateful for his love and support.

To all my mentors - I have had the good fortune of working with some extremely competent and kind people during my professional journey who had a profound impact on my personality - some of them became close friends over time. While its impossible to mention all names here but two names that stand out as I reflect on my journey are - Sanjay Berry (my first boss during my internship days) and Samit Bhat (my senior during internship and later at KPMG) - Both of them are very dear friends now & their personalities had a huge influence on my life. Their ability to forge & invest in relationships is inspirational. I remain grateful for their love, support & guidance during my formative years.

To my friends and readers, who shared their stories of saving, struggle, and success — your journeys inspired many of the reflections in this book.

A heartfelt thanks to my editor and publishing team for shaping the manuscript with care and precision and for believing in the message of financial empowerment.

Finally, to every reader who chooses to take charge of their financial life — this book is dedicated to you.

May this book inspire you to see money not just as currency, but as a tool for Freedom of Choice and catapult your journey towards a life of peace & purpose.

ABOUT THE AUTHOR

Hitesh K. Pahuja is a Chartered Accountant and Company Secretary with 25 years of experience in the corporate sector. He has worked in multiple countries, including India, and in his last role, he was the CEO for the India Business of a large MNC.

Hitesh started his career with Bharat Petroleum (a Fortune 500 company) in Mumbai and, over the years, worked with names like KPMG, Vedanta Group, Renew Power, and Fluence India. During a career spanning 25 years, Hitesh has worked in multiple functions as well as with multiple nationalities, which contributed to his development journey.

Hitesh is passionate about personal finance, financial literacy, and financial freedom. He intends to share his experience with the generations younger than him with the objective to help them avoid the mistakes he made and work on some of the financial behaviours he found useful in his own journey.

This book is his first formal attempt to share knowledge with the younger generation, and he intends to engage with the readers through this. He endeavours to devote some part of his time to educating the younger generation about the basics of finance and believes this is still poorly appreciated, as a life skill, by many.

In his free time, Hitesh loves to travel to the mountains and read. Hitesh lives in Gurgaon with his family and can be reached at Hitesh Kumar | LinkedIn.